The French liner *Paris* at Le Havre, heeled over on her port side after a fire. See p. 25.

DOOMED SHIPS
Great Ocean Liner Disasters

WILLIAM H. MILLER, Jr.

DOVER PUBLICATIONS, INC.
Mineola, New York

For Stanley Lehrer
World-Class Nautical Collector
First-Class Maritime Historian
Beloved Friend & Mentor

Bibliographical Note

Doomed Ships: Great Ocean Liner Disasters is a new work,
first published by Dover Publications, Inc., in 2006.

Library of Congress Cataloging-in-Publication Data

Miller, William, H., 1948–
     Doomed ships : great ocean liner disasters / William H. Miller, Jr.
         p. cm.
     Includes bibliographical references and index.
     ISBN 0-486-45366-9 (pbk.)
       1. Shipwrecks. 2. Ocean liners. 3. Ocean travel. I. Title.
     G525.M51 2006
     363.12'31—dc22

                                                                  2006048460

Book design by Carol Belanger Grafton

Manufactured in the United States of America
Dover Publications, Inc., 31 East 2nd Street, Mineola, N.Y. 11501

FOREWORD

With dozens of books to his credit, ship historian and author Bill Miller has rendered a great service to ocean liner history. The vanished seagoing icons live on, in large part, through his works. This particular volume focuses on passenger vessels crossed by tragedy, starting with the *Lusitania*, torpedoed in 1915, and continuing all the way through the foundering in China of the 1960-built *Oriana* in 2005. Most ships lead uneventful lives, serving their owners for decades until being recycled. Some are less lucky, however, and are consumed by neglect, war, sabotage, and/or accident. Names like *Morro Castle*, *Andrea Doria*, and *Lakonia* have become synonymous with disaster. These high-profile ships took their human tolls, and received worldwide attention, and yet there are many other ill-fated ships that are equally interesting, but perhaps a bit more obscure. This book covers both well-known and less-familiar doomed ships.

Achille Lauro, "La Nave Bleu," the former *Willem Ruys*, was my home for a twelve-night Mediterranean adventure out of Genoa in October of 1994, a few short weeks before her end. From the bridge, with its panels still displaying bullet holes from the ship's notorious 1985 terrorist hijacking, down to its sleek, tumble-homed waterline, the ship was quirky and magnificent. Among other ships I have known...Costa Line's *Carla C*, the ex–French Line *Flandre* of 1952, was like a well-worn Italian shoe, but so homey and with the warmest staff and crew. Another time I spent a scorching afternoon documenting the aged features of Paradise Cruises' *Romantica* in Piraeus. Months later, I was viewing her charred hulk from a hired boat off Limassol, Cyprus. These three wonderful old ladies all met fiery ends, which will be detailed in these pages.

Some of my favorite ships, like the 1931-built *Britanis* (ex-*Monterey*), slipped away more quietly, succumbing to swelling seas at the end of a towrope. The *Britanis* was an extraordinary survivor, with brass promenade windows, teak decks, and 1950s Hawaiian decor. I was fortunate enough to sail in her twice and pay many visits, even during the ship's final, derelict days at Tampa. Nearby lay the *Sea*, another forgotten and similarly fated liner, whose faded black funnels and gutted, corroding superstructure were a far cry from the sparkling Swedish American liner *Gripsholm* I visited as a child. The crumbling, 1940-built *Alferdoss* had sat neglected at her Eleusis anchorage for nearly thirteen years by the time I clambered aboard in 1992. The former *America*, she was a magnificent Art Deco icon filled with original artwork and furnishings from her transatlantic glory days. I found the *Sun* (ex-*Shalom*) languishing at Freeport in 2000. She was but an empty shell, save for her stair towers, which featured priceless original art panels by Yaacov Agam. Among the saddest and most dreary ships I have ever encountered was the abandoned *Copa Casino* (ex-*Ryndam*) at a Mobile, Alabama shipyard. She was listing so badly that the doors in her waterlogged alleyways hung open, blocking passage, and her cinema was flooded. In December 1994, while sailing past the lava flows of Kilauea onboard American Hawaii's *Constitution*, it seemed as though the ship's twin funnels and wonderfully archaic counter stern would go on forever. They would not, as you will soon read.

My personal list is merely the tip of the proverbial iceberg of fascinating ships covered in this wonderful book. The alarm is sounding! It is time to gather your life jacket and proceed directly to your muster station. Many interesting ships, their stories, and their harrowing fates are ready to unfold.

PETER KNEGO
Moorpark, California
January 2006

ACKNOWLEDGMENTS

Once again, many hands, including "the crew," have been involved in the compilation of this book. Anecdotes and photos were collected, sorted, and then worked into the project. As expected, locating support material for some of the ships proved more challenging than others. I remain most grateful to so many friends, who, in kindness, generosity, and often with great patience, were ready to assist. Together we believe that passenger ships—particularly bygone ones—must be kept alive. Documentation in books is one of the very best ways to do this. And so, we are most grateful to Dover Publications for suggesting this title. Dover produces excellent, high-quality, affordable books. My association with them, which began in 1979, happily continues. The connection started with the late Hayward Cirker, the founder of Dover, at the company's former offices located in lower Manhattan on Varick Street. Sparked by his own Atlantic crossings by liner in the 1930s, Mr. Cirker was intrigued by maritime topics. Thanks to his interest and foresight, we have produced some twenty books together. I am especially grateful to the present staff at Dover (now in Mineola, Long Island): Clarence Strowbridge, for suggesting new titles and accepting others; Suzanne E. Johnson, for her editorial skills and great sense of accuracy and detail; and Carol Belanger Grafton, for her splendid design and layout.

Apart from Dover, "the crew" is really quite sizeable. I am particularly grateful to Richard Faber for providing photographs and other materials for all of my books, and to Peter Knego for his thoughtful Foreword and his much-appreciated support, photographs, and personal recollections. Also, the highest praises to Abe Michaelson, my business partner, who promotes, sells, and distributes books to the four corners of the earth. In addition, my warmest thanks to the late Frank Andrews, Ernest Arroyo, Frank Braynard, Philippe Brebant, J. K. Byass, Michael Cassar, Tom Cassidy, Anthony Cooke, Luis Miguel Correia, the late Frank Cronican, Arthur Crook, Frank Duffy, the late Alex Duncan, Maurizio Eliseo, James and Tina Flood, the late John Gillespie, Dr. Nico Guns, Andy Hernandez, Charles Howland, Bob Kemelhor, Arnold Kludas, Bard Kolltviet, Stan Lehrer, Robert Lenzer, Victor Marinelli, Captain James McNamara, Richard Morse, Carl Netherland-Brown, Hisashi Noma, Robert Pelletier, Paolo Piccione, Fred Rodriguez, Rich Romano, Jurgen Saupe, Roger Scozzafava, the late Antonio Scrimali, James L. Shaw, Captain Ed Squire, Steven Tacey, Frank Trumbour, the late Everett Viez, Al Wilhelmi, Steven Winograd, Hans Jurgen Witthoft, James Wheeler, V. H. Young, and L. A. Sawyer.

Firms and organizations that greatly assisted include British India Line, Carmania Press Limited, Carnival Cruise Lines, Celebrity Cruises, Crystal Cruises, Cunard Line, Hapag-Lloyd, Hoboken Historical Museum, Moran Towing & Transportation Company, the Ocean Liner Council at the South Street Seaport Museum, Port Authority of New York & New Jersey, Radisson–Seven Seas Cruises, Royal Mail Lines, South China Morning Post, Steamship Historical Society of America (especially the Long Island Chapter), the U.S. Merchant Marine Museum, World Ocean & Cruise Society, and the World Ship Society (most notably the Port of New York Branch). There are also companies that are, alas, no more, such as Bethlehem Steel Company and Flying Camera, Inc. If I have failed to mention anyone else, my great apologies. But know that you are all well appreciated and have assisted in keeping a part of our maritime history alive.

INTRODUCTION

The idea for this particular title was put forward by Dover Publications itself. Usually, *I* would propose the title and the content, always with an eye on readily available photographs. Dover felt strongly about the subject of doomed passenger liners, but suggested we avoid the already heavily documented *Titanic*, which sank following a collision with an iceberg in the western Atlantic on April 15, 1912. They decided on beginning the book with another, very famous British liner disaster, the sinking of the *Lusitania* on May 7, 1915. And so, being in full agreement, we had our starting point, our launch of sorts. There have been many passenger ship disasters since then, of course. Quite simply, there have been far too many. Including them all, however, would have greatly exceeded the page allotment for this title. And quite obviously, during the very destructive years of the Second World War, between 1939 and 1945, the sheer number of ships destroyed required that only the more notable tragedies be included. One-third of the world's passenger ship fleet was destroyed during those grim times. There has been some emphasis, however, on more recent tragedies, those since the 1960s, which involve some liners sinking on their very last voyages, bound for Middle- and Far-Eastern scrap yards.

The final complete list herein is actually quite interesting. The *Lusitania*, the *Morro Castle*, the *Normandie*, and the *Andrea Doria* are among the most famous doomed ships and their stories have been frequently recounted in books, lectures, television documentaries, and specialized videos. As I pen this work, there are at least two major books in the works, one on the celebrated, innovative *Normandie*, and another on Italy's postwar flagship, the *Andrea Doria*. It seems there is always more to be written, more to be learned, more perhaps to question and ponder over in the matter of maritime misfortunes. Other disasters of note are included here as well, which doomed such ships as the *Europa*, *L'Atlantique*, *President Hoover*, *Berengaria*, *Empress of Britain*, *Viceroy of India*, *Rex*, *Wilhelm Gustloff*, *Yarmouth Castle*, *Leonardo da Vinci*, *Achille Lauro*, and the *Oriana*.

Sometimes the strange workings of fate bring about surprising coincidences. Soon after I began planning for this book—outlining, making lists, organizing the first file folders, and assembling the photos (noting gaps and weak spots)—I headed off, in October 2005, on a one-month voyage to the Orient. Booked a year in advance, I was one of the guest lecturers onboard one of the world's finest cruise ships, the *Seven Seas Mariner*, a contemporary floating palace with an all-suite configuration, walk-in closets, and marble tubs. There were complimentary select wines at dinner and separate grill rooms featuring French and Asian delicacies. In the six-star league, we were very pampered guests living like seagoing royalty. By coincidence, among my 700 or so fellow passengers, two of them had direct connections to noted ships and their tragic endings. Their first-person recollections of the burning of the *Morro Castle* in 1934 and the salvage of the fire-gutted *Normandie* in 1942–43 are included in the following pages. I interviewed both parties, who were happily agreeable to share their stories over luncheon tables, and I soon felt a stronger connection to my title. Yes, this book was, as one might say, "picking up steam and gaining speed." I was off and running.

Although still a schoolboy in 1956, I well recall the black-and-white television images of the sinking of the *Andrea Doria* on July 26. It was the very first maritime tragedy of note brought into the homes of America and the world. In near disbelief, we could see this grand ship, well known to New York harbor buffs such as myself, capsizing gradually to starboard and then sinking beneath the waves of the western Atlantic off Nantucket. The final sights were the most dramatic, perhaps even horrifying, as the stern section and an exposed propeller, part of the underbelly of the 700-foot liner, poked above those otherwise sun-splashed waters for the last time. Then, as it sank, there was a turbulence, a flourish—the last breath and sigh of a doomed vessel. Debris filled the waters, some of it in a washing machine-like swirl. The *Andrea Doria* was gone—she was officially dead. Because she had been an extremely familiar sight along New York's Luxury Liner Row and reputedly one of the safest liners yet built, I could not bring myself to believe she had sunk, even after buying the daily newspapers with their blazing headlines of the liner's loss, which reinforced those television news films and photos. I asked my father to take me by car from our home in Hoboken to the cliffs of nearby Weehawken for a better view of the West Side liner piers in Manhattan. It was Friday, July 27, and I was sure that it was all *incorrect*, that the *Andrea Doria* would be at her regular berth at Pier 84, at West 44th Street. She could not have really sunk—so I thought. But, of course, the slip was empty, lonely, sad, and desolate.

As if to reinforce it all further, I could see the little, all-white Swedish *Stockholm*, now securely berthed at Pier 97, some thirteen blocks north at West 57th Street. She was being called the "villain," the ship that sank the splendid, larger *Andrea Doria* in a collision on the foggy night of the 25th. As the *Stockholm* lay there still and quiet, the damage she had sustained was quite apparent. I could see that her raked bow was missing, the fore portion gutted and smashed from ramming the *Andrea Doria*. The small, 12,000-ton *Stockholm* was outbound at the time of the tragedy, headed on an otherwise typical summer's voyage to Scandinavia, while the 29,000-ton *Andrea Doria* was just completing a crossing from the western Mediterranean, only hours away from her arrival in New York harbor. The shock of the collision and the loss of the Italian liner lingered in the public mind for some time. Stories were featured in *Life*, *Look*, *Newsweek*, and the ever-fascinating *Popular Mechanics*, of ways in which the *Andrea Doria*, resting on the bottom on her starboard side, could be raised, salvaged, and later repaired.

Filling her hull with thousands of Ping-Pong balls was one of the curious ideas. Dragging her on shore with huge chains was another. It all made, of course, for fascinating and fanciful reading. Later, in December 2005 as I busily prepared this book, our Ocean Liner Council at New York's South Street Seaport Museum was laying plans for an all-day, Saturday salute six months away, in June, to the still-alluring *Andrea Doria*. Lectures, slide shows, exhibits of artifacts and memorabilia, and even accounts from survivors, as well as divers who had investigated the wreck, were included. The event would finish off with a celebratory dinner in one of Manhattan's Italian restaurants. The festivities were thoughtfully dubbed, Italian Dreamboat: The *Andrea Doria*.

But back to that Asian cruise in October 2005. Our first stop in China was Dalian, once part of old Manchuria and now a teeming city of skyscrapers, shopping malls, high-rise apartments, and amusement parks. It is also a very busy seaport. As we arrived in the first, soft light of day, I hurried to an open upper deck. My purpose: to spot the remains of the former P&O liner *Oriana*, the last liner mentioned in these pages. Partially capsized during a typhoon the year before, she was finally righted, but reports of repair and restoration proved false for the forty-five-year-old liner. By the summer of 2005 it was reported that she would be scrapped locally, perhaps at one of the large, nearby shipyards. China has, of course, the largest need anywhere in the world for recycled steel. But my top-deck investigation came to nothing. She was nowhere to be seen. Once ashore, about to board a tour bus waiting on the dockside, I came across some harbor officials. They knew of the former *Oriana*, of course, but told me that she had been towed away and demolished in another Chinese port, at remote Jiangsu. And so, what might have been a link to the last of the passenger ships listed herein proved illusive.

Nevertheless, the list remains very interesting. Great ships, often with busy lives, tending to their passengers and crew, and providing crucial global links, have sometimes ended in tragedy. Fires, torpedoes, collisions, desperate calls of SOS and requests for lifeboats, heroic rescues and daring escapes, blaring newspaper headlines and formal inquiries. These are all elements in the fascinating stories recounted here of *Doomed Ships: Great Ocean Liner Disasters*.

BILL MILLER
Secaucus, New Jersey
Winter 2005–06

PHOTO CREDITS

LUSITANIA. The *Lusitania* came from the golden age of Atlantic liners. She was a true superliner, a near sister to the immensely successful, long-lived, and thoroughly beloved *Mauretania*, which sailed from 1907 until 1934. The latter ship had further claim to fame: she held the coveted Blue Riband for transoceanic speed for twenty-two years (1907 until 1929). Launched at the illustrious John Brown yard along Scotland's River Clyde, the "Lucy," as she was dubbed, entered service in September 1907 and briefly captured the Blue Riband herself. She sailed in the Cunard Line's main express service, crossing between Liverpool and New York in six days. She is seen here (*above*) at Cunard's West 14th Street pier in Manhattan. Capped by four towering funnels, she was typically class-divided for her time. This view (*below*) showing her first-class lounge hints of her finer luxuries.

Popular, well run, and a true North Atlantic favorite, the *Lusitania* became known for her part in one of the greatest ocean disasters. Hers was a wartime tragedy in the first dark year of World War I, the "war that was to end all wars." The *Lusitania* was considered for alternative military service from her inception, and was given a secret refit in 1913—a year before the war began. Her foredecks were fitted with magazines (storage areas for ammunition). When war was officially declared in August 1914, the British Admiralty enlisted the *Lusitania* as an armed auxiliary cruiser. At the same time, she continued her peacetime service, sailing on monthly round-trip voyages between New York and Liverpool. Her sailings lasted into 1915, even after the Germans openly announced that all shipping around the British Isles was liable to attack. Nevertheless, the giant *Lusitania* steamed on, carrying "regular" passengers, as well as supposed "general cargo."

On May 1, 1915, she sailed from New York's Pier 54, at the foot of West 14th Street, with 1,533 passengers and 1,400 tons of "freight," including 1,248 concealed cases of three-inch shrapnel shells and 4,927 boxes of cartridges. After an otherwise uneventful voyage, she reached the Irish coast on the sixth, and received Admiralty radio warnings of German submarine activity in the area. Such notices did not seem to apply, as the *Lusitania* was an "unarmed passenger liner." But onboard safety precautions were taken just the same, including keeping the numerous lifeboats in readiness, and the closure of most watertight doors and bulkheads.

The German Navy had suspicions, however, about the true nature of the ship's cargo, and ordered one of its submarines, the *U-20*, to sink either the *Mauretania* or *Lusitania*, two of Britain's finest and best-known liners. On the otherwise quiet afternoon of May 7, a German submarine sighted the *Lusitania*, clearly visible in the bright midday sunshine. The first torpedo was fired at 2:10 P.M., and struck the ship's starboard side just below the bridge. There was prompt flooding and an immediate fifteen-degree list. A second torpedo was at first thought to have been fired, but, it was actually the explosion of the ammunition in the foredeck magazines. The giant ship was mortally wounded, and flooded so quickly that she sank off the Old Head of Kinsale, near Queenstown (today Cobh), Ireland, within eighteen minutes. The losses were horrific: 1,159 passengers and 702 crew perished. Only 374 passengers and 289 crew survived.

Many survivors later protested that the Cunard Line was at fault, and that there was chaos among the officers, and negligence, further complicated by an inexperienced crew. Cunard was officially cleared at the conclusion of inquiries in August 1918, and the blame for the incident laid on the German government. Over the years, there have been several undersea expeditions to the famed Cunard liner. Captain Carl Netherland-Brown recalled one from the late 1980s. "There was an expedition financed by a rich Texan, an attempt to secure such items as the anchor, bell, whistles, and propellers, which went terribly wrong. The dive team used far too many explosives and caused great damage to the wreckage. The explosions even jolted the research ship above. Much of the *Lusitania*'s stern was destroyed. It was such a regrettable situation and, in the end, nothing was taken." [Built by John Brown & Company Limited, Clydebank, Scotland, 1907. 31,550 gross tons; 787 feet long; 87 feet wide. Steam turbines, quadruple screw. Service speed 25 knots. 2,165 passengers (563 first class, 464 second class, 1,138 third class).]

KRISTIANAFJORD. It might have been seen as an unlucky start. The *Kristianafjord* was the first ship in the new Norwegian America Line and carried the King of Norway, his ministers, and other officials on an inaugural coastal voyage from Christiana to Bergen in June 1913. She is seen here *(above)* on her maiden departure from Oslo. Afterward, the flag-bedecked liner set off on her maiden crossing to New York with 906 passengers onboard. Unfortunately, navigation proved hazardous and the *Kristianafjord* ran aground near Mistaken Point, some seven miles from Cape Race, Newfoundland. While the passengers and crew were rescued, the otherwise brand-new ship was abandoned as a complete loss. [Built by Cammell, Laird & Company Limited, Birkenhead, England, 1913. 10,669 gross tons; 530 feet long; 61 feet wide. Steam quadruple-expansion engines, twin screw. Service speed 15 knots. 1,017 passengers (101 first class, 216 second class, 700 third class).]

CITY OF HONOLULU (ex-*Friedrich der Grosse*). Before being renamed the *City of Honolulu* in 1922, this ship had been a transatlantic liner, North German Lloyd's *Friedrich der Grosse*, completed in late 1896. After World War I was declared in August 1914, she was left at the company's piers in Hoboken, New Jersey. She remained idle until seized by the U.S. Navy in April 1917 just as the United States officially entered the hostilities. The *City of Honolulu* then became the troopship USS *Huron*. In 1922, she was handed over to private owners, the Los Angeles Steamship Company (LASSCO), for use on the Los Angeles–Honolulu run. Unfortunately, her remaining days were brief. She is seen here *(opposite, top)* docked in Los Angeles harbor. On her return maiden voyage on October 12, 1922, she caught fire in the eastern Pacific and burned completely. Five days later the burned-out hulk was deliberately sunk by gunfire from a U.S. Navy vessel. [Built by Vulcan Shipyard, Stettin, Germany, 1896. 10,771 gross tons; 546 feet long; 60 feet wide. Steam quadruple-expansion engines, twin screw. Service speed 15 knots. 244 all-first-class passengers.]

FONTAINEBLEU. Messageries Maritimes, based in Marseilles, was the second largest of the great French passenger lines. In addition to the French Line's celebrated transatlantic service to North America, Messageries Maritimes serviced more far-flung routes: from France to Africa, the Middle and Far East; and to the Pacific, including Australia. For their Far Eastern run, which included calls at Singapore, Saigon, Manila, Hong Kong, Kobe, and Yokohama, the company added the *Fontainebleu (opposite, middle)* in the late summer of 1924. Hardly a noteworthy ship, she was one of a good number of Messageries Maritimes' passenger ships that finished her days by fire. On July 12, 1926, off Djibouti en route to the East, she caught fire and burned completely. Her wreckage was subsequently sunk to form a local breakwater. [Built by Ateliers et Chantiers de la Loire, St. Nazaire, France, 1924. 10,015 gross tons; 501 feet long; 59 feet wide. Steam geared turbines, twin screw. Service speed 15 knots. 576 passengers (130 first class, 80 second class, 116 third class, 250 steerage).]

PRINCIPESA MAFALDA. Navigazione Generale Italiana (NGI) was one of Italy's great early passenger lines, offering almost worldwide service. One of their finest ships, the twin-funnel *Principesa Mafalda* plied the South American run, from Naples to Rio de Janeiro, Montevideo, and Buenos Aires. Seen here *(opposite, bottom)* in an artist's rendering, she had been acquired through a merger with another Italian ship owner, Lloyd Italiano, in 1918. Her end came on October 25, 1927, when, approaching the Brazilian coast, a port propeller shaft broke, which allowed flooding and caused boilers to explode in the engine room. Panic erupted as the ship began to list. Within four hours she capsized, taking 303 souls with her. [Built by Societa Esercizio Bacini, Riva Trigoso, Italy, 1909. 9,210 gross tons; 485 feet long; 56 feet wide. Steam quadruple-expansion engines, twin screw. Service speed 16 knots. 1,700 passengers in first and third class.]

VESTRIS. Britain's Lamport & Holt Line ran a popular service from New York to the Caribbean and then down along the east coast of South America to Rio de Janeiro, Santos, Montevideo, and finally Buenos Aires. The *Vestris (above)* and her sisters *Vasari*, *Vandyck*, and *Vauban* were fine passenger-cargo liners on this service and were especially popular for winter vacation voyages. However, it was the *Vestris* that changed the fortunes of the Liverpool-based company. After departing from New York on November 10, 1928, the single-stacker encountered very heavy weather off the coast of Virginia, prompting her cargo to shift, and thereby creating an increasingly worrisome list. An SOS was sent and both passengers and crew began to evacuate, but not before sixty-eight passengers and forty-four crew members perished when she finally capsized. The survivors were rescued by several nearby ships, including two passenger vessels: the *American Shipper* of United States Lines and the *Berlin* of North German Lloyd. The effect of this disaster, coupled with the Wall Street crash in October 1929, prompted Lamport & Holt to discontinue all New York passenger service in 1930. [Built by Workman, Clark & Company, Belfast, Northern Ireland, 1912. 10,494 gross tons; 511 feet long; 61 feet wide. Steam quadruple-expansion engines, twin screw. Service speed 15 knots. 610 passengers (280 first class, 130 second class, 200 third class).]

CELTIC. The *Celtic* and her sister *Cedric* were the largest liners in the world when they were completed in 1901. They were the White Star Line's premier ships, sailing on the company's express run between Liverpool and New York. Later joined by the similar-looking *Adriatic* and *Baltic* (of 1906), they formed the "Big Four," sailing weekly in each direction. They were eclipsed in size, speed, and luxury by three new superliners, beginning with the *Olympic* (1911), the *Titanic* (1912), and the *Britannic* (1914). The *Celtic* is seen here *(below)* in New York's Lower Bay.

During World War I, the *Celtic* suffered two damaging incidents: she hit a mine in the Irish Sea in February 1917 and had to be towed to Liverpool for repairs. Then, in March 1918, she hit another mine in the Irish Sea and was sent to Belfast for repairs. But her final fate came a decade later, on December 10, 1928. She was entering Queenstown harbor during a seventy-miles-per-hour gale, carrying a scant 254 passengers, including twenty-five survivors from the aforementioned *Vestris* disaster, when a violent gust of wind sent her on the rocks at Roche's Point. Water flooded the engine room through a gaping hole. The *Celtic* had to be grounded. The passengers and crew were brought ashore by tenders and the twenty-seven-year-old ship was declared a complete loss. Valued at $1.5 million, she was sold to a Copenhagen-based salvage company, which scrapped her on the spot. The process took five years, ending in 1933. [Built by Harland & Wolff Limited, Belfast, Northern Ireland, 1901. 20,904 gross tons; 700 feet long; 75 feet wide. Steam quadruple-expansion engines, twin screw. Service speed 16 knots. 2,857 passengers (347 first class, 160 second class, 2,350 steerage).]

PAUL LECAT. The *Paul Lecat* (**above**), like the *Fontainebleu*, was also used on the Messageries Maritimes' Far East service. The ship caught fire in homeport waters at Marseilles on December 30, 1928. Burning for almost two days, she was a complete loss in the end and was quickly sold to nearby Italian ship breakers at La Spezia. [Built by Constructions Navales, La Ciotat, France, 1911. 12,989 gross tons; 529 feet long; 58 feet wide. Steam quadruple-expansion engines, twin screw. Service speed 15 knots. 1,274 passengers (194 first class, 145 second class, 109 third class, 826 steerage).]

FORT VICTORIA. Something of a pioneer "tourist ship" in the very popular New York–Bermuda trade, the *Fort Victoria* (**below**) began her sailing days as a Pacific passenger-cargo ship, the *Willochra*. Owned by the Union Steamship Company, she traded between New Zealand, Australia, the U.S. west coast, and Vancouver. Used as a transport in World War I, she was sold after the armistice in 1919 to London-based Furness, Withy & Company, which had varied shipping interests, among them the Furness-Bermuda Line. She was renamed *Fort Victoria* for weekly New York–Bermuda sailings.

On December 18, 1929, the single-funnel ship made a customary departure from New York's Pier 95, but was forced to stop in thick fog just outside the port at the entrance to Ambrose Channel. Sounding her whistle continuously, she was nonetheless rammed by an inbound passenger ship, the Clyde Lines' *Algonquin*, and seriously damaged, with flooding. All passengers and crew were saved, but the ship slipped beneath the Atlantic later that evening. [Built by William Beardmore & Company, Glasgow, Scotland, 1913. 7,784 gross tons; 412 feet long; 57 feet wide. Steam quadruple-expansion engines, twin screw. Service speed 16 knots. 429 passengers (373 first class, 56 second class).]

MONTE CERVANTES. Its ships capped by distinctive red-and-white funnels, the Hamburg–South America Line was well known for its liner services between northern Europe and the east coast of South America. Calling at ports in Portugal and Spain en route, the ships were sometimes fitted for low-fare immigrants bound for new lives in Brazil, Uruguay, and Argentina. Between 1924 and 1931, five sister ships were built especially for this trade. The third one was the *Monte Cervantes*. While normally used on the South American run, she and her sisters also ran occasional, off-season, low-fare cruises from Hamburg as well as Buenos Aires.

On January 22, 1930, the twin-funnel *Monte Cervantes* was on a cruise, sailing from Buenos Aires to the Straits of Magellan when she ran aground on some uncharted, submerged rocks in the Beagle Channel *(above)*. The ship began to sink, the passengers and crew were evacuated, and the ship was deliberately driven onto a nearby reef. The attempt to save her failed, however, and the ship capsized, claiming the life of the captain. German maritime historian and author Hans Jurgen Witthoft added, "The *Monte Cervantes* capsized so suddenly that Captain Dreyer, who had remained onboard, could not be rescued. He went under with his ship, the only person to be lost. A well-earned honor was bestowed posthumously on Dreyer, an excellent seaman whom all witnesses of the accident credited with faultless behavior and whose reactions and decisions were expressly approved by the court of inquiry. A Kapitan-Dreyer-Weg was named after him in the Hamburg district of Blankenese." The ship's remains were not salvaged until 1951. The salvage operation was completed three years later; however, the hulk of the *Monte Cervantes* sank while under tow. [Built by Blohm & Voss Shipbuilders, Hamburg, Germany, 1928. 13,913 gross tons; 524 feet long; 66 feet wide. MAN diesels, twin screw. Service speed 14 knots. 2,492 passengers (1,354 tourist class, 1,138 steerage).]

CITY OF HONOLULU (ex-Kiautschhou). Dockside fires can be devastating. The *City of Honolulu*, built as Hamburg America Line's *Kiautschou* and then transferred to North German Lloyd, where it became the *Prinzess Alice*, was an early Pacific cruise ship. Seized by the Americans during the World War I, she became the troopship *Princess Matoika*, then a commercial transatlantic liner until laid up in 1923. The Los Angeles Steamship Company bought her in 1926 and refitted her as the *City of Honolulu* for the Los Angeles–Honolulu service beginning in June 1927 *(below)*. She caught fire at her Honolulu berth on May 25, 1930, and was burned out. She was able, however, to sail under her own power to Los Angeles for repairs, but ideas for restoration were rethought. Laid up for a time, she was sold to Japanese ship breakers in 1933. [Built by A. G. Vulkan, Stettin, Germany, 1900. 10,860 gross tons; 540 feet long; 60 feet wide. Steam quadruple-expansion engines, twin screw. Service speed 17 knots. 495 passengers (445 first class, 50 third class).]

EUROPA. German author Hans Jurgen Witthoft wrote of the *Europa* fire: "The alarm bells shrilled at about 3:30 A.M. on the night of March 25 to 26, 1929. A fire had broken out as the liner sat beneath the large hammerhead crane at the Blohm & Voss shipyard in Hamburg. It quickly spread, becoming a devastating conflagration that largely destroyed the completion work the ship had undergone in previous months. The shipyard as well as city fire brigades were called into action. There were eventually 350 firemen battling the fire with sixty-five hoses. However, the water could not flow out of the *Europa* fast enough, and she developed an almost instant fifteen-degree list to starboard. An attempt had to be made to ground the ship to prevent her from capsizing with the high tide in the morning. What resulted was that the *Europa* was more of a wreck than a ship. But her future was assessed and repairs made. While the cause of the fire could never be clearly established, the damage caused onboard the *Europa* was the largest claim settled at any time for the ship's broker, M. W. Joost, a long-standing partner of Blohm & Voss in insurance matters. Joost responded quickly: it made out a check for the sum of 18,222,564 marks on July 25, 1929." These two views show the blaze from the bridge (*above*) and the twisted steel along the upper decks (*below*).

The *Europa* was one of the greatest liners of the twentieth century. She had two separate careers, one for the Germans and one for the French, and was nearly lost twice. Finally completed a year late in March 1930, the *Europa* took the prized Blue Riband for speed from her near-sister *Bremen* on her maiden run to New York. She is seen here (*above*) at a later date with her flat funnels raised in height in a floating dock at Hamburg. Not used during the Second World War, she was seized by the invading American forces at Bremerhaven in May 1945 and began a short stint as the troopship USS *Europa*. But fires caused by faulty fittings prompted the US government to give the liner to the French as reparations. Renamed *Liberté*, she was nearly lost when, on December 8, 1946, she was ripped away from her moorings at Le Havre and then ran into the sunken wreckage of the *Paris*. This view (*below*), dated December 9, shows the former German liner torn from her Le Havre berth with the wreckage of the *Paris* to the right. The news caption identified the former *Europa* at this point as *La Liberté*. The *Liberté* quickly sank and was not raised until April 15. Seen here, repaired and refitted, (*opposite, top*) in a St. Nazaire shipyard in 1950, she sailed for the French Line until late 1961 and then was sold to Italian ship breakers. [Built by Blohm & Voss Shipbuilders, Hamburg, Germany, 1930. 49,746 gross tons; 936 feet long; 102 feet wide. Steam turbines, quadruple screw. Service speed 27 knots. 2,024 passengers (687 first class, 524 second class, 306 tourist class, 507 third class).]

MUNCHEN. Used on North German Lloyd's run between Bremerhaven, Southampton, Cherbourg, and New York, this ship was nearly lost when she caught fire on February 11, 1930, at Pier 42 in Greenwich Village, New York City. Smoke from the burning ship spread across the city. She was salvaged as seen here *(below)* on April 3, and sailed under her own power on May 9 for repairs in Germany. She reemerged as the *General von Steuben* and in 1938 was rechristened *Steuben.* Used as an accommodation ship by the Nazis during the war, she was called to evacuation duty in the winter of 1945. With 2,500 wounded, 2,000 refugees, and 450 crew onboard, she left Pillau in Poland for Kiel on February 9. A day later she was sunk by a Soviet sub. An estimated 3,000 people perished. [Built by Vulkan Shipyard, Stettin, Germany, 1923. 13,325 gross tons; 551 feet long; 65 feet wide. Steam triple-expansion engines, twin screw. Service speed 15 knots. 1,079 passengers (171 first class, 350 second class, 558 third class).]

HIGHLAND HOPE. The *Highland Hope* was barely a year old when she was destroyed. Completed in January 1930, she was one of six sisters built for Britain's Nelson Line for their passenger and freight service from London to the east coast of South America. On a southbound voyage that November, she grounded on the Farilhoes Rocks, off the Portuguese coast, was abandoned, and declared a complete loss. An identical sister, the *Highland Chieftain*, is shown in this aerial view *(above)*. [Built by Harland & Wolff Limited, Govan, Scotland, 1930. 14,129 gross tons; 544 feet long; 69 feet wide. Burmeister & Wain diesel, twin screw. Service speed 15 knots. 701 passengers (135 first class, 66 second class, 500 third class).]

BERMUDA. The *Bermuda* was a pioneer luxury cruise ship that did a great deal to popularize New York–Bermuda sailings. She was big, well decorated, and instantly successful, but her career was all too brief. Completed in January 1928, the ship later undertook a cruise to Bermuda on June 17, 1931. On this voyage, tragedy struck. She is seen here *(opposite, bottom)* during her maiden arrival at Hamilton, Bermuda. After two fires broke out in the early morning hours, the ship was soon abandoned and began to list at her Hamilton berth. The damage was limited to the superstructure, so she was pumped out and then sailed a month later for repairs at Belfast. But further misfortune was ahead. While at the shipyard, on November 19, 1931, a far more serious fire engulfed the ship *(above)* and caused her to sink. She was raised five weeks later and found to be a complete loss *(below)*. Sold to scrappers in Rosyth, Scotland, she was under tow, but then ran aground in the Badcall Islands and ended up a total wreck. The *Bermuda* must be counted as having one of the most unlucky careers of any passenger ship. [Built by Workman, Clark & Company, Belfast, Northern Ireland, 1927. 19,086 gross tons; 547 feet long; 74 feet wide. Doxford diesels, quadruple screw. Service speed 17 knots. 691 passengers (616 first class, 75 second class).]

GEORGES PHILIPPAR. In the 1930s especially, fire plagued French passenger ships, including the *Georges Philippar*. This new ship was in fact a replacement for the aforementioned, fire-damaged *Paul Lecat*, another Messageries Maritimes passenger ship used on the Marseilles–Suez–Far East service. In fact, the *Georges Philippar* had a serious fire while fitting out in January 1932 and became the subject of an investigation by the French secret police. After entering service that April, her maiden voyage was marked by a cloud of suspicion, including the possibility that she was carrying munitions for the Japanese invasion of China. On May 15, while approaching the Gulf of Aden on her return from this voyage, fire broke out in her passenger areas, as seen here (*above*) in a midday view. The captain attempted to increase speed to port, but this only helped spread the blaze. The ship was soon abandoned. There were fifty-four casualties during the evacuation process. The *Georges Philippar* burned for four days and drifted 160 miles until she finally sank on May 19. By then, she was the sixth Messageries Maritimes ship to be lost to fire and the second lost on her maiden voyage. [Built by Ateliers et Chantiers de la Loire, St. Nazaire, France, 1931. 17,539 gross tons; 567 feet long; 68 feet wide. Sulzer diesels, twin screw. Service speed 15 knots. 1,045 passengers (196 first class, 110 second class, 89 third class, 650 steerage).]

PIETER CORNELISZOON HOOFT. Like the *Georges Philippar* (previous plate), this French-built ship had a fire while fitting out, but then was repaired. "Two separate fires broke out, both due to short circuits," notes Dr. Nico Guns, one of Holland's foremost passenger ship historians and authors. Built for Holland's Nederland Line for their Amsterdam–East Indies service, the ship's career also proved to be rather brief. On November 14, 1932, the six-year-old vessel burned out at her Amsterdam berth. Beyond repair, she was towed to the outer harbor and sold to local Dutch ship breakers. "While at her Amsterdam berth, during the execution of cyanogen fumigation for the extermination of the ship's vermin, a huge fire broke out," writes Dr. Guns. "Fiercely burning for nine days, she drifted on the River IJ. While being towed to the scrap yard, she caught fire once more, nearly capsized, ran aground and then broke adrift. When finally at the scrapper's dock, she was gutted by fire once more. She then sank and had to be raised before scrapping could start." The ship is shown here (*opposite, bottom*) during safer times. [Built by Ateliers et Chantiers de la Loire, St. Nazaire, France, 1926. 14,729 gross tons; 549 feet long; 67 feet wide. Sulzer diesels, twin screw. Service speed 17.5 knots. 639 passengers (205 first class, 273 second class, 107 third class, 54 fourth class).]

L'ATLANTIQUE. The *L'Atlantique* was the largest liner ever built for the Europe–South America run. She was one of the great "dreamboats" of the 1930s, and a first cousin to the innovative, ever-popular *Ile de France*. "The superb interiors of this ship were the pacesetters for the *Normandie*," according to ocean liner historian and collector Steven Winograd. "She was a cross between Art Nouveau and Art Deco, connecting the past with the present. It was, of course, the end of Nouveau. Among ships, she was the link between the *Paris* and the *Normandie*. On the outside, she was not as attractive. The funnels, both the original smaller ones and then the larger replacements, were wrong. But she was mighty, reading like 80,000 tons in a 40,000-ton hull."

But the doomed *L'Atlantique* was destroyed while still almost a new ship. She is shown here (*above*) with her raised funnels. Introduced in September 1931 she was on a voyage without passengers, sailing from Bordeaux to Le Havre on January 4, 1933, when fire broke out in a passenger cabin and then quickly spread. Rapidly abandoned, the liner burned for two days and then drifted toward the Dorset coastline. Unfortunately, seventeen crewmembers were lost during the incident.

Put under tow by French, German, and Dutch seagoing tugs on January 6, *(opposite, top)* she was brought to Cherbourg to await her fate *(opposite, middle)*. Later, following intense studies, the ship's owners, Compagnie Sud-Atlantique, claimed her to be a complete loss and fixed her value at close to $8 million. The underwriter claimed she could be repaired by Harland & Wolff of Belfast for approximately $5 million *(opposite, bottom)*. The owners finally won out, but only after the gutted, rusting ship laid at Cherbourg until sold to Glasgow scrappers in 1936. Steven Winograd added, "The insurance companies had to pay in the end, but only after a long, dragged-out battle. She was a wreck, forty percent burned out, sixty percent damaged. Her demise led, of course, to the smaller, refined *Pasteur* of 1939." [Built by Chantiers de l'Atlantique, St. Nazaire, France, 1931. 42,512 gross tons; 742 feet long; 92 feet wide. Steam turbines, quadruple screw. Service speed 21 knots. 1,156 passengers (414 first class, 158 second class, 584 third class).]

DRESDEN. Completed in 1915 as North German Lloyd's *Zeppelin*, the brand-new ship sat unused throughout World War I and then was given to Britain as reparations, becoming the *Ormuz* of the London-based Orient Line. Repurchased by North German Lloyd in 1927, however, she became the *Dresden*, used on transatlantic crossings to New York as well as on Nazi party "Strength through Joy" cruises in the 1930s. It was on one of these voyages, to the Norwegian fjords, on June 20, 1934, that she struck a submerged rock off Karmoe Island and began to flood. She later capsized *(above)* and was quickly declared a complete loss. [Built by Bremer-Vulkan Shipyard, Vegesack, Germany, 1915. 14,690 gross tons; 570 feet long; 67 feet wide. Steam quadruple-expansion engines, twin screw. Service speed 15.5 knots. 971 passengers (399 cabin class, 288 tourist class, 284 third class).]

MORRO CASTLE. The tragic end of the *Morro Castle* made endless headlines and was widely covered in newsreels and movie theaters. Her demise shocked Americans, and changed safety standards for U.S.-flag vessels thereafter. "The fire and subsequent loss of the *Morro Castle* not only changed Coast Guard safety regulations in the United States, but also the rules of marine insurance writing," noted Captain James McNamara.

One of the finest of a new generation of American liners built in the early 1930s, the *Morro Castle* and her sister, the *Oriente*, were designed for the very popular New York–Havana cruise trade. Capped by twin funnels, they were miniature Atlantic liners in almost all ways. It was on the *Morro Castle*'s return from Havana, on September 8, 1934, that misfortune stalked the ship. First, the captain died that night of a heart attack; then there was a fire in the writing room, a blaze that soon raged out of control *(opposite, top)*. The crew seemed less than properly prepared to fight the flames and winds fanned the fire. The SOS call was made too late and soon passengers began to panic. Later, passengers complained of never having had a lifeboat or safety drill, and inquiries found some crew to be incompetent. In all, 137 lives were lost as the *Morro Castle* burned off the north end of the New Jersey coast. A day later, the still-burning ship drifted onto the beach at Asbury Park and became a public spectacle *(opposite, bottom)*. The ship was subsequently found to be improperly equipped, manned by a poorly trained crew and a staff suffering from low morale. Lawsuits amounted to a staggering $13.5 million and the blistered remains of the ship were sold off to Baltimore scrappers. She is shown here *(above)* arriving under tow.

"My grandparents went down to Asbury Park just after the fire and saw the smoldering liner on the beach," recalled Steven Winograd. "They bought photos colored with red crayons to look like the flames, which sold for fifteen cents each. The *Morro Castle* and her tragedy belong to New Jersey history as well as New York history. The Ward Line was negligent, of course, and had to settle out of court. Long after they were out of the shipping business, their name lived on at an old pier at the foot of Spring Street in Lower Manhattan, which stood there until the early 1980s." [Built by Newport News Shipbuilding & Dry Dock Company, Newport News, Virginia, 1930. 11,520 gross tons; 530 feet long; 70 feet wide. Steam turbo-electric, twin screw. Service speed 20 knots. 530 passengers (430 first class, 100 tourist class).]

DORIC. Despite the sad circumstances of the *Doric's* loss, the decline of passenger traffic during the Depression era of the 1930s probably made the Cunard–White Star Line somewhat relieved to have one less passenger ship. An Atlantic liner, the *Doric* began losing regular passengers after 1930 and was subsequently used as an all-one-class, discount cruise ship. It was on a Mediterranean cruise, on September 5, 1935, when the homeward bound *Doric (above)* collided with the 2,100-ton French freighter *Formigny* off Cape Finisterre, Spain. The liner was ripped open at the waterline, but managed to remain afloat. Her 735 passengers and crew were soon transferred to two nearby liners, the *Orion* and the *Viceroy of India*. The *Doric* was repaired at Vigo and later sailed for London, but she was badly damaged and Cunard eventually sold her to ship breakers in Wales. In all, her career lasted twelve years. [Built by Harland &

Wolff Limited, Belfast, Northern Ireland, 1923. 16,484 gross tons; 601 feet long; 67 feet wide. Steam turbines, twin screw. Service speed 15 knots. 2,300 passengers (600 first class, 1,700 third class).]

AUSONIA. The small liner *Ausonia* was used in Lloyd Triestino's inter-Mediterranean service between Italy, Palestine, and Egypt. Upon arrival at Alexandria on October 18, 1935, a boiler explosion started a fire and the ship was soon abandoned *(below)*. Destroyed beyond repair, she was towed to Trieste and broken up. [Built by Ansaldo Shipyards, Genoa, Italy, 1928. 12,955 gross tons; 544 feet long; 66 feet wide. Steam geared turbines, twin screw. Service speed 20 knots. 390 passengers (210 first class, 120 second class, 60 third class).]

CRISTOBAL COLON. The Spanish Line, Compania Trasatlantica Espanola, maintained a rather unique, triangular transatlantic service: from Spain across to New York and then southward to the Caribbean and Central America. The *Cristobal Colon* was one of the largest passenger ships used on this run *(above)*. At the outbreak of the Spanish Civil War in August 1936, she was diverted to England, but was refused permission to land. She then went to France and finally home to Spain, where she wound up in the hands of Leftists. By October, however, Franco sympathizers gained control of her and she fled for Mexico with only sixty-five crewmembers onboard. Unfortunately, a miscalculation caused her to be wrecked on East North Rock, just north of Bermuda, on October 24. The ship was abandoned and declared a complete loss. This scene of the wreckage *(below)* dates from August 1941. [Built by Societa Espanola de Construccion Naval, Ferrol, Spain, 1923. 10,833 gross tons; 520 feet long; 61 feet wide. Steam geared turbines, twin screw. Service speed 16 knots. 1,100 passengers in three classes.]

PRESIDENT HOOVER. Following the tragic demise of the *Morro Castle*, the loss of the *President Hoover* was another blow to the virtually new American passenger ship fleet of the 1930s. She was only six years old when she was lost. The *President Hoover* is shown here *(opposite, top)* in San Francisco harbor on her maiden arrival. She and her sister, the *President Coolidge*, were two of the finest liners in Pacific service and ran between San Francisco and Yokohama, Kobe, Manila, Hong Kong, and Shanghai. "The *President Hoover* was the quintessential American liner of the 1930s," according to Frank Trumbour, a world-class ocean liner collector and former chairman of the Ocean Liner Museum in New York. "Her dollar sign insignia (representing the Dollar Line) was somewhat ironic in the age of the Great Depression. Nevertheless, she was a handsome vessel both inside and out."

While en route between Kobe and Manila on December 10, 1937, with over 1,000 passengers and crew onboard, she ran aground on Hoishito Island, a Japanese territory near Taiwan. She was abandoned, and after several attempts to refloat her, the ship was declared a complete loss and sold to Japanese ship breakers. [Built by Newport News Shipbuilding & Drydock Company, Newport News, Virginia, 1931. 21,936 gross tons; 654 feet long; 81 feet wide. Steam turbo-electric engines, twin screw. Service speed 20 knots. 988 passengers (307 first class, 133 tourist class, 170 third class, 378 steerage).]

BERENGARIA. Old age for ships has long been a problem for shipping lines. The mechanics, including the wiring, begin to wear out and problems arise: breakdowns, delays, and, worst of all—fires. The *Berengaria* was one of the great favorites of 1920s travel on the North Atlantic. This 52,100-tonner was Cunard's largest liner until the *Queen Mary* first appeared in 1936. She had been awarded to the company as reparations, having been Hamburg America's *Imperator*, completed in 1913, and a near sister to the subsequent but larger still *Vaterland (Leviathan)* and *Bismarck (Majestic)*. She was used on Cunard's "Big Three" express, partnered with the *Aquitania* and the *Mauretania*. She was, however, a great victim of the lean Depression years. Cunard began to send her on short, inexpensive cruises, from New York down to Bermuda, and on long weekends up to Halifax. With her luxurious Atlantic days seemingly past, she was dubbed the "Bargain-area." Steven Winograd added, "She was a great favorite and looked so much better, a true showstopper, in her Cunard days. Unlike the *Mauretania* and *Aquitania*, she was unique in being named for a person (a 13th-century English queen) rather than a place (Roman provinces). She might just have been the most singularly popular big liner of the 1920s. She was a great 'now' ship and passengers booked suites and cabins aboard her years in advance."

After Cunard merged with White Star in 1934, the *Berengaria's* fate, like that of so many other Cunarders, fell into greater question. For a time, she sailed with the brand-new *Queen Mary*, but only as a temporary mate. The older ship is seen here *(opposite, bottom)* in New York's Lower Bay. She might have lasted through 1939, just as the *Queen Elizabeth* came into service in the spring of 1940, but old age did her in first. In 1938 small fires plagued her, caused mostly by aged wiring. At one point, the U.S. Coast Guard refused her a sailing permit from New York. The *Berengaria* was sold to ship breakers in Scotland soon afterward. Her final pieces actually survived World War II and were not cut up until 1946. [Built by Bremer Vulkan Shipyards, Hamburg, Germany, 1913. 52,226 gross tons; 919 feet long; 98 feet wide. Steam turbines, quadruple screw. Service speed 23 knots. 2,723 passengers in 1921 (972 first class, 630 second class, 606 third class, 515 tourist class).]

LAFAYETTE. In the short span of four years, The French Line, one of the North Atlantic's most prestigious and popular passenger lines, suffered the devastating loss of four of their finest liners. First the *Lafayette* in May 1938, then the *Paris* in April 1939, the *Champlain* in June 1940, and, possibly most devastating of all, the magnificent *Normandie* in February 1942.

The French Line built a succession of fine liners, beginning with the *Paris* of 1921, as a prelude to the record-breaking *Normandie* of 1935. The *Ile de France* first appeared in 1927, the smaller *Lafayette* in 1930 *(below)* in New York's Lower Bay on her maiden arrival, and two years later the *Champlain*. The *Lafayette* was lying in dry dock at Le Havre on May 4, 1938, when a fire erupted in the provision area and spread quickly. Within three hours, the liner was blazing from end to end and was soon declared a complete loss. Her twisted, badly burned remains were towed away to Rotterdam for scrapping. [Built by Chantiers de l'Atlantique, St. Nazaire, France, 1930. 25,178 gross tons; 613 feet long; 77 feet wide. MAN diesels, twin screw. Service speed 17 knots. 1,079 passengers (583 cabin class, 388 tourist class, 108 third class).]

RELIANCE. The Nazi regime was embarrassed over the loss of the *Reliance*. This fine Hamburg America liner was lost to fire in Hamburg harbor no less. She was one of Nazi Germany's finest cruise ships of the 1920s and '30s. The *Reliance* had been built originally as the *Johann Heinrich Burchard*, but her construction was halted during World War I. After some difficulties she was handed over to the Royal Holland Lloyd in 1920, but was renamed *Limburgia*. Unsuccessful on the Europe–South America run, she joined the United America Lines in 1922, became the *Reliance* and, uniquely for that time, flew the Panamanian colors, today a very popular "flag of convenience." Hamburg America Line bought back their ship in 1926, but retained the name *Reliance*. She was used for crossings as well as cruises, such as in this view *(above)* in Norway. On August 7, 1938, as she was about to sail on a summer cruise to Scandinavia, the ship caught fire at her Hamburg berth. The *Reliance* was declared a complete loss and in 1941 her remains were sold to Krupp for scrapping. [Built by J. C. Tecklenborg Shipyard, Geestemunde, Germany, 1920. 19,582 gross tons; 615 feet long; 71 feet wide. Steam triple-expansion engines, triple screw. Service speed 16 knots. 1,010 passengers (290 first class, 320 second class, 400 third class).]

PARIS. "The *Paris* was an innovative ship. She literally said good-bye to the past and hello to the future. She did away with the heavy interiors of the past, such as on the *France* of 1912," according to Steven Winograd. "She was modernistic. She had Art Nouveau and even Moroccan styles and lavish glass and metalwork. She was actually the first French liner to look forward. And her exterior was interesting, with the clustered three funnels placed far forward." The *Paris* is seen here *(opposite, top)* in an aerial view, outbound in New York harbor in 1928.

"For me, the *Paris* was notable for her interiors," said Charles Howland, a major collector and expert on ocean liners. "She was decorated in the curvaceous Art Nouveau style. Her design phase was from 1914 to 1915, and her interiors reflect that period, not the later Art Deco style of the mid 1920s. It is fair to say, however, that the French Line had decided to say good-bye to the eighteenth-century Louis style that characterized the *France* of 1912. Management made the decision to look to modern trends in interior decor. It was not necessarily a safe decision, but a gutsy one." The ship's splendid, two-deck-high, first-class dining room is shown in this view *(opposite, bottom)*.

Howland added, "Whenever I think of the *Paris*, I think of that marvelous French Line poster of the ship racing through the Atlantic, lights blazing. What an evocative image of a chic French liner! She had the misfortune to suffer serious fires twice in her career. First, in 1929, when her accommodations were pretty much ruined, and then in 1939, when she burned, capsized and sank at her berth."

The *Paris* was one of the Atlantic run's most distinguished and popular liners. In 1939, along with her regular passengers and some general cargo, the *Paris* was loading French treasures for display in the New York World's Fair. Sadly, the proud liner never left her Le Havre berth on that scheduled sailing. On April 19 she caught fire and heeled over on her port side the following day *(opposite, top and bottom)*. Her masts had to be cut almost immediately since she was blocking the giant *Normandie* from safely leaving the large graving dock (dry dock) at Le Havre *(above)*. She was a complete loss, but her wreck sat untouched throughout the war years and was not scrapped until 1947. [Built by Chantiers de l'Atlantique, St. Nazaire, France, 1921. 34,569 gross tons; 764 feet long; 85 feet wide. Steam turbines, quadruple screw. Service speed 22 knots. 1,930 passengers (560 first class, 530 second class, 840 third class).]

MAJESTIC. The *Majestic* was aged, creaking, and well past her prime. A last attempt to find a use for her proved unfortunate. Intended to be the third of Hamburg America Line's super liners, she was named *Bismarck*, launched in June 1914, but then laid up unused during World War II. Seized by the Allies after the war, she was handed to the British as reparations and completed as the *Majestic* for the White Star Line. According to many sources, she ranked as the largest liner afloat, from 1922 until 1935. The giant ship is seen here (*above, left*) in a poetic view as she arrives at night in the floating dry dock at Southampton in 1926. Decommissioned in February 1936 she was soon sold for scrap, but then resold to the British Admiralty for use as a stationary training ship for 2,000 cadets. Renamed *Caledonia*, she burned at her moorings at Rosyth, Scotland, on September 29, 1939, and then sank in rather shallow water. She was later broken up between 1940 and 1943. [Built by Blohm & Voss Shipbuilders, Hamburg, Germany, 1914–22. 56,551 gross tons; 950 feet long; 100 feet wide; 35-foot draft. Steam turbines, quadruple screw. Service speed 23.5 knots. 2,145 passengers (750 first class, 545 second class, 850 third class).]

COLUMBUS. "The *Columbus* was a rather ordinary looking vessel, but of course the first big liner to be built following the devastation of the German fleet in World War I," according to Frank Trumbour. "There was little to distinguish her. The shortening of her funnels in 1929 gave her a look of speed and sleekness that previously eluded her." The *Columbus* is shown here (*above, right*)

departing from New York's Pier 86 on a winter cruise in 1936. She was also used in North German Lloyd's "big ship" express service between Bremerhaven and New York, together with the larger, faster, and grander *Bremen* and *Europa*. In August of 1939 the *Columbus* was on a Caribbean cruise just as World War II was about to start in Europe. Her American passengers were put ashore at Havana and the liner fled to neutral safety at Vera Cruz, Mexico. The Nazi regime ordered her return to home waters, and on December 14 she was intercepted off the Virginia coast by a British warship. To avoid capture, the *Columbus* was deliberately scuttled. The crew set her on fire and her sea cocks were opened. On December 19 she sank 320 miles east of Cape Hatteras and ranked as the first major ship loss for the Nazis during World War II. This view (*opposite*) of Manhattan's Luxury Liner Row on a Saturday morning in February 1939 shows the *Columbus* in happier times. From top to bottom are the *Monarch of Bermuda* and the *Fort Townshend*, Furness-Bermuda Line; the *Conte di Savoia*, Italian Line; the *Aquitania* and *Britannic*, Cunard–White Star; the *Normandie* and *De Grasse*, French Line; the *Bremen* and *Columbus*, North German Lloyd; and finally the *Hamburg*, Hamburg American Line. All but the *Fort Townshend, Aquitania*, and *Britannic* would endure tragedy. [Built by Schichau Shipyards, Danzig, Germany, 1924. 32,581 gross tons; 775 feet long; 83 feet wide; 36-foot draft. Steam turbines, twin screw. Service speed 23 knots. 1,725 passengers (479 cabin class, 644 tourist class, 602 third class).]

ATHENIA. Created for the Glasgow-Montreal service of Britain's Donaldson Line, the *Athenia* (*above*) was the first U-boat victim of World War II. While on a civilian voyage to Canada on September 3, 1939, she was torpedoed some 200 nautical miles off the Hebrides, with the loss of 112 people. Aware of the policy at that time that no action should be taken against passenger ships, the Nazis quickly denied responsibility. [Built by Fairfield Shipbuilding & Engineering Company Limited, Glasgow, Scotland, 1923. 13,465 gross tons; 538 feet long; 66 feet wide. Steam turbines, twin screw. Service speed 15 knots. 1,516 passengers (516 cabin class, 1,000 third class).]

OSLOFJORD. In some ways, the *Oslofjord* was one of the war's saddest losses. She was only two years old when she sank. Handsome on the outside and smartly appointed within, she was the pride of the Norwegian America Line. She is shown here (*below*) docking at the line's terminal, located at the Brooklyn Army Terminal in New York's Lower Bay, on September 14, 1939. Used as an Allied troopship beginning in October 1940, she was lost to a mine two months later, on December 1 at the mouth of England's River Tyne. [Built by A/G Weser Shipbuilders, Bremen, Germany, 1938. 18,673 gross tons; 590 feet long; 73 feet wide. MAN diesels, twin screw. Service speed 19.5 knots. 860 passengers (152 first class, 307 tourist class, 401 third class).]

STATENDAM. The flagship of the Holland America Line, the *Statendam* is shown here *(above)* on her maiden voyage in May 1929. This three-stacker was caught in crossfire at her Rotterdam berth during the Nazi invasion of Holland in May 1940. The *Statendam* burned for five days *(below)*, a symbol of the horrific destruction of war, the collapse of the Netherlands, and the reality of the Nazi occupation. Her wreckage was scrapped locally in the summer of 1940. [Built by Harland & Wolff Limited, Belfast, Northern Ireland, 1921–27; completed by Rotterdam Dry Dock Company, Rotterdam, Holland, 1927–29. 29,511 gross tons; 697 feet long; 81 feet long. Steam turbines, twin screw. Service speed 19 knots. 1,654 passengers (510 first class, 344 second class, 374 tourist class, 426 third class).]

CHAMPLAIN. If the *Champlain* had not returned to Europe from New York after World War II began in September 1939, she might have survived the conflict. Built at St. Nazaire, the 28,100-ton *Champlain* made her debut on the Le Havre–New York run in June 1932. The 641-foot-long ship looked quite modern for her time. In this 1939 view **(above)**, she sits across from the *Normandie* at French Line's Pier 88 in Manhattan, capped by a funnel that had been heightened considerably. "She was, of course, a test ship for the forthcoming *Normandie* of 1935. She had the same uncluttered decks, the modern funnel, the mast above the wheelhouse," said Everett Viez. "She was typically French modern for the 1930s. But later, when that funnel was raised in height, her good looks were spoiled somewhat. She was also a follow-up to the diesel-driven *Lafayette*, which had operational problems, and so the *Champlain* reverted to steam turbines."

Unfortunately, the *Champlain* was an early war casualty. On June 17, 1940, she struck a mine and sank off western France with the loss of 330 lives. Rather amazingly, it took eighteen years, from 1946 until 1964, to fully salvage and scrap her remains. [Built by Chantiers de l'Atlantique, St. Nazaire, France, 1932. 28,124 gross tons; 641 feet long; 82 feet wide. Steam turbines, twin screw. Service speed 19 knots. 1,053 passengers (623 first class, 308 tourist class, 122 third class).]

ARANDORA STAR. The *Arandora Star* was one of the finest cruise ships of her day. Built for Britain's Blue Star Line in 1927, she started out as a combination passenger-cargo ship, the *Arandora*, making the run from London to the east coast of South America (*above*). A year later, she had the first of many refits that made her one of Britain's finest and most popular cruise ships of the 1930s. Retaining her original name, she offered superb accommodations for 354 all-first-class passengers. She sailed to the Mediterranean, West Africa, Scandinavia, the Baltic capitals, around the British Isles, and crossed in winter to the Caribbean. Renamed the *Arandora Star* in 1929, she was one of the earliest ships to call at Miami, then an infant Florida port, but today the cruise ship capital. Unfortunately, the 15,500-ton *Arandora Star* was an early wartime loss. While serving as a converted trooper, she was torpedoed off Ireland by a German submarine on July 2, 1940, with the tragic loss of 761 souls. [Built by Cammell, Laird & Company Limited, Birkenhead, England, 1927. 15,501 gross tons; 535 feet long; 68 feet wide. Steam turbines, twin screw. Service speed 16 knots. 354 all-first-class passengers.]

LANCASTRIA. In 1940, Winston Churchill, then First Lord of the Admiralty, ordered that the sinking of the *Lancastria* and her horrifying loss of life be kept secret because of its staggering and possibly demoralizing effect on the Allied war effort. Intended for the Anchor Line, but bought by Cunard before completion, the ship was first named *Tyrrhenia*, but that name proved unpopular and was changed in 1924 to *Lancastria* (*below*). On June 16, 1940 she was at St. Nazaire, serving as a troopship helping evacuate western France. Loaded with an estimated 5,500 passengers, she was attacked by Nazi bombers. The *Lancastria* suffered four serious hits (including one down her funnel) and sank within twenty minutes. Official estimates were that 3,000 perished—the worst catastrophe in maritime history—but subsequent reports suggested that 9,000 might have been onboard and that 5,000 perished. Churchill ordered that news of the loss be delayed by a month and that losses be put at 2,500. [Built by William Beardmore & Company Limited, Glasgow, Scotland, 1922. 16,243 gross tons; 578 feet long; 70 feet wide. Steam turbines, twin screw. Service speed 16 knots. 1,785 passengers (265 first class, 370 second class, 1,150 third class).]

EMPRESS OF BRITAIN. The *Empress of Britain* was the largest Allied liner lost during World War II. Built in Britain for service to the British Dominion of Canada, she entered service in May 1931, uniquely designed for that time as a dual-purpose ship: Atlantic crossings for about eight months of the year and then cruises—usually a four-month trip around the world—for the remainder. On the Atlantic, she carried 1,195 travelers in three classes (very spacious for a ship of that size) and then only a club-like 700 passengers for wintertime circumnavigation. The round-the-world voyages began with the ship sailing outward from New York to the Mediterranean and then through Suez, and homeward across the Pacific and through the Panama Canal. The cost of these trips started at about $2,000 in the financially hard-pressed '30s. The ship is seen here *(above)* at Balboa, Panama. Despite her popularity, her great size, and her overall luxury and grandeur, the *Empress of Britain* was a great money loser both on the Atlantic as well as in cruising. She was simply too big for either service. Any thought of a sister or a running mate was soon forgotten by her disappointed owners. In 1946, after the war, the British government suggested a replacement, but Canadian Pacific directors politely declined it.

Charles Howland was a great fan of this Canadian Pacific super liner. He said, "I have a warm spot for the *Empress of Britain*. If any ship shouted ocean liner, she did! Traditional lines, oversized funnels, and with glamorous, but at the same time warm, Art Deco interiors. Her career was too short and her end was tragic."

"I especially liked Canadian Pacific interiors. They were all maple leaves and sycamores," said Steven Winograd. "The *Empress*

of Britain was the best Canadian Pacific liner of all. She was all scrolled carpets and cream-colored columns. And I loved her look with the three massive funnels. She was the last of the truly inspired liners of the 1920s. It was a great pity that she never earned a dime."

In June 1939 she carried King George VI and Queen Elizabeth home from their friendship-building North American tour to Canada and the United States. Queen Mary, Princess Elizabeth (today, the Queen), and Princess Margaret were at the Southampton docks to greet their parents and the flag-bedecked Canadian Pacific flagship. "I've often thought that her role in bringing the King and Queen of England home after their state visits to Canada and the United States was hugely symbolic. She presented such a strong and forthright profile. She seemed to typify the strength of the ties between Britain and North America. Certainly the Germans must have been aware of her symbolic value when they sank her," noted Charles Howland.

In the fall of 1939, months after the royal voyage, the *Empress* was called to war duty for use as a troopship. This service was quite brief, however. While homebound from South Africa, the ship was attacked by Nazi bombers off the Irish coast on October 26, 1940. Burning but still afloat, *(opposite, top and bottom)* she was attacked two days later by an enemy sub. She sank with forty-nine casualties. [Built by John Brown & Company Limited, Clydebank, Scotland, 1931. 42,348 gross tons; 758 feet long; 97 feet wide. Steam turbines, quadruple screw. Service speed 24 knots. 1,195 passengers (465 first class, 260 tourist class, 470 third class).]

BREMEN. If fate and strategies had been different, the *Bremen* might have been retained in New York harbor, later seized and used as an Allied troopship. In this view (*above*) from November 16, 1938, police keep protesters carrying anti-Nazi banners away from the *Bremen*'s midnight sailing from New York's Pier 86. She eventually returned to Nazi Germany in the fall of 1939 and never sailed again. She is seen here (*below*) leaving New York for the last time, on August 30, 1939, with the brand-new American liner *Panama* to the right. The *Bremen* was, of course, one of the greatest German liners of the twentieth century—a record breaker, speed champion, and a near-sister to the *Europa*. A true ocean greyhound with squat funnels, which were soon raised, she was completed in July 1929 for express service between Bremerhaven and New York, with stops at Southampton and Cherbourg en route.

"The *Bremen*'s lines suggested speed and her seaplane [resting in a revolving catapult on the top deck] suggested the latest and the fastest in communication," noted Frank Trumbour. "Her interiors were Spartan, but sophisticated, from her Hollywood-like cigar stand to her beautiful staircases. The silver background of the mosaic on the walls of its anteroom must have created a glamorous feeling as one approached the chic ballroom with its illuminated fountain." Charles Howland added, "The *Bremen* was a fast, powerful, and efficient expression of national pride in Germany. Apart from her record-breaking maiden voyage, however, I guess her last dash home to Germany at the start of World War II was her most memorable trip—one fraught with danger and a close encounter with a British sub." She was laid up at Bremerhaven from December 1939 and then set on fire by an unhappy, anti-Nazi youth in March 1941. Completely burned out, she was later scrapped. [Built by A/G Weser Shipbuilders, Bremen, Germany, 1929. 51,656 gross tons; 938 feet long; 102 feet wide. Steam turbines, quadruple screw. Service speed 27 knots. 2,200 passengers (800 first class, 500 second class, 300 tourist class, 600 third class).]

NORMANDIE. To some, the loss of the magnificent *Normandie* was one of the worst maritime tragedies of World War II. Some still call the French flagship the most luxurious liner of all time. She is shown here sailing on her eastbound maiden voyage, departing from Pier 88 in New York (*above*).

The ship's Art Deco interiors were legendary, as seen in these views of her smoking room *(above)* and first-class main dining room *(below)*. She was also a very advanced ship, a record-breaking ship, but also a short-lived ship. The *Normandie* was the fastest vessel afloat for a time and commissioned in May 1935, but then abruptly decommissioned in August 1939, just as World War II exploded in Europe. She sat at Pier 88, at the foot of West 48th Street, for over two years until in December 1941 she was seized as a prize of war by the U.S. government. She was earmarked for conversion to a much-needed, high-capacity troop transport, the USS *Lafayette*.

Unusually, her transformation was conducted at her Manhattan berth rather than at an over-crowded shipyard. But haste led to carelessness, and on the cold afternoon of February 9, 1942, the 1,028-foot-long super liner caught fire *(opposite, top and bottom, and page 38, top and bottom)*.

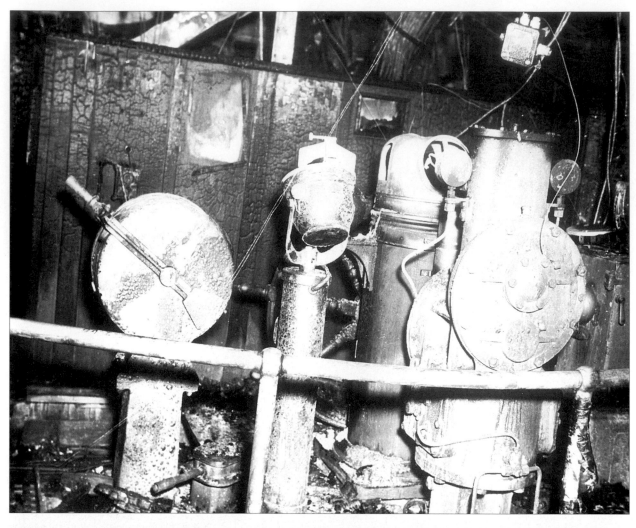

In the ensuing fire fighting efforts, she was overloaded with water and capsized on her port side (*above*). A devastating loss to the war effort, she appeared to be, as one onlooker recalled, "like a big, dead whale." Another dubbed her a "goddess in ruins."

"The *Normandie* was known to be a fragile ship, in fact a very fragile ship," according to Captain James McNamara. "The Navy actually held off using her until 1942 when, desperate for big troop transports, they decided to convert her for the Australian run. But they knew she had very risky stability. This led, of course, to her capsizing so easily and quickly in the subsequent fire in New York."

"It is hard to write about the *Normandie* and her needless destruction," added Charles Howland. "She was a victim of carelessness, stubbornness, and just plain stupidity. It is easy to place the blame, but hard to accept what happened. First, there was the carelessness of the worker whose acetylene torch set fire to thou-

sands of kapok life vests. Then there was the stubbornness of the U.S. Navy admiral who wouldn't let the ship's designer, Vladimir Yourkevitch, onboard to open the sea cocks—a solution which would have allowed the ship to settle on an even keel. Then there was the stupidity of continuing to pump tons of water onto the ship's upper decks, which destroyed her stability. Like most disasters, a series of incidents contributed to the ultimate destruction of the ship. For me, the *Normandie* is the great 'if only.' If only the worker had been more careful. If only the French crew had been onboard to operate the fire control system. If only the admiral had allowed Yourkevitch to open the sea cocks. If only the fireboats had stopped pumping sooner. If only, if only! Still, the *Normandie* will always be the standard by which all subsequent super liners are judged. For that, and for her extraordinary beauty, we must be grateful."

Bob Kemelhor was a diving specialist for the U.S. Navy in Washington. He was soon assigned to the salvage of the *Normandie*, a most difficult and pressing project in those otherwise hectic wartime years. "She had rolled over to seventy-nine degrees," he recalled as we cruised China's Yellow Sea together aboard another French-built liner, Radisson's splendid *Seven Seas Mariner*, in the fall of 2005. Here we see (*above*) the nighttime salvage view dated March 27, 1942. "I was assigned to coordinate the navy divers, about forty to fifty of them, who were, in fact, being trained for subsequent work in clearing Pearl Harbor, plus the private salvage contractors, the crews from New York harbor–based Merritt, Chapman & Scott. The *Normandie* had a racing hull, an hourglass hull. This complicated her stability. I was sent to New York within days of the fire and boarded the ship through a plank. There was one plank forward and one aft, and I recall entering through the cargo openings. I felt sad, very sad. The fire and the loss of the *Normandie* was one of the biggest mistakes in U.S. naval history and also one of the biggest mistakes made by the New York City Fire Department. By the day of the fire, everything had been removed from the first-class ballroom, to be replaced by stacked kapok lifejackets for 15,000 soldier-passengers that she would begin carrying within a few weeks in Allied troop service. The mirrors and chandeliers had not been removed, however. These would later become great hazards. The glass shattered and cut the divers and their suits. The kapok jackets had arrived three days early and were stored in the ballroom area.

The welding to remove fittings was not yet complete. Kapok is, of course, very flammable. The lifejackets needed to be isolated and kept in fireproof chambers. And so, the fire started when sparks from a welder's torch ignited those kapok jackets. Soon, four or five fireboats and then land equipment indiscriminately poured water on the *Normandie*. She was a burning ship and a ship with a fragile hull. Smoke filled the ship and caused further chaos. But while the fire was serious, it was not fatally destructive. The fire could have been fought successfully and the ship ultimately saved. But the fire was fought from the outside. And in this, there was both disorder and miscalculation."

On February 10, just after 2:00 A.M., the *Normandie* rolled over and capsized. In the gray light of the next morning, the ship was a grotesque sight. "She was lying on her port side, resting on a rock ledge," added Kemelhor. "Initially, the plan was to pump her out and then let the hull refloat itself. There was great optimism that she could be saved and then used for the war, but the load placed pressure on the keel, and the keel was unable to take the bending load. The keel bent and, as it was soon discovered, the ship could not be salvaged and returned to service. The first inspections showed at least a year of pumping would be required. Initially, it was planned to seal all the portholes and replace them with wood coverings, and then seal the entire ship. But further investigations proved that she was not salvageable and we finally resolved that she was best suited to become nothing more than 'steel toothpicks.'"

Bob Kemelhor organized and scheduled the dive crews. "The mood at first was 'gung ho' to save the ship at all costs," he said. "There was even a plan to use cranes and concrete stanchions on Pier 88 to right the ship. Merritt, Chapman & Scott had 'old-time' divers, who were both experienced and tough. They chewed tobacco, wore old suits, and used vintage equipment. Onboard the capsized Normandie, it was very dark. The divers came back with anything and everything, including furniture, china, and works of art, and tried to salvage the most valuable fittings. Eventually, we put lights onboard. The stench was another problem, but each morning we seemed to get more accustomed to it. She would also rock slightly with the tidal changes of the Hudson. It was the biggest salvage operation in history and we worked twenty-four hours a day. It was, of course, a very big task, but then just really a part of the overall war effort. Of course, it was also a horrible sight and a very emotional thing to many of us. I still vividly remember the Normandie."

This view (*above*) is from August 8, 1943.

The Normandie was cut down and finally righted in November 1943, towed to Brooklyn's Columbia Street pier, laid up, and then declared surplus in 1946, after the war ended. Her scarred hull was sold later to the Lipsett Scrap Metals Company for a mere $161,000 and then broken up in Port Newark, New Jersey in 1947, where her hull is seen (*below*) being dismantled that summer.

Steven Winograd offered a rather poetic theory on why so many French liners were lost to fire. "French liners were so beautiful. They burned bright, but they burned hot," he said. "Their food, decor, elegance, and style were all too good. And anything that good can't last. French liners were simply too good!" [Built by Chantiers de l'Atlantique, St. Nazaire, France, 1935. 82,799 gross tons; 1,028 feet long; 117 feet wide. Steam turbo-electric engines, quadruple screw. Service speed 29 knots. 1,972 passengers (848 first class, 670 tourist class, 454 third class)].

GEORGIC. The *Georgic* was the last passenger ship to be built for the White Star Line, which, by 1932, had fallen on hard financial times. Within two years, ships such as the 27,700-ton *Georgic* were part of the merged Cunard–White Star companies. Together with her near-sister *Britannic*, she plied the New York trade from Liverpool, as well as London, and did considerable cruising. After becoming a troopship in 1940 (*left*) the *Georgic*'s career was scarred. She was bombed, set afire, and very badly damaged during a German air attack on Port Tewfik, Egypt, on July 14, 1941. The subsequent salvage and long rehabilitation, which reduced her to a single-stacker (as seen in this view [*below*] of the ship arriving at Capetown), lasted until 1944, after which she became a permanent trooper and postwar migrant ship. Cunard used her until 1955, but only for summer season, low-fare, all-tourist-class service. Because of lingering wartime damage, the *Georgic* was not permitted to sail the North Atlantic in winter, but instead made trips to Australia. She was scrapped in Scotland in 1956. [Built by Harland & Wolff Limited, Belfast, Northern Ireland, 1932. 27,759 gross tons; 711 feet long; 82 feet wide. Burmeister & Wain diesels, twin screw. Service speed 18 knots. 1,542 passengers as built (479 cabin class, 557 tourist class, 506 third class)].

WAKEFIELD. Like the *Georgic*, the former *Manhattan* might have been lost, given up due to high damages, but she too was repaired, restored, and gave further Allied war service. Together with her sister *Washington*, the *Manhattan* was the largest new American liner on the North Atlantic in the 1930s. Owned by United States Lines, she sailed in commercial service until called to war duties in 1941. The ship is seen here *(above)* preparing for a midnight sailing from New York's Pier 61, in 1939. The *Manhattan* was refitted as the transport USS *Wakefield*. She caught fire, however, on September 3, 1942, while in a westbound North Atlantic convoy. Abandoned at first, she was later recovered and brought into Halifax and then Boston. Totally repaired and extensively rebuilt, she resumed service some eighteen months later in May 1944. She is shown in New York harbor in this view *(below)* from the summer of 1945, with her decks lined with returning troops. Two years later, she was decommissioned and laid up in the U.S. government's "mothball fleet" in the upper Hudson River near Bear Mountain, New York. Finally surplus in 1964, she was sold for scrap and delivered to Kearny, New Jersey, ship breakers in March 1965. [Built by New York Shipbuilding Company, Camden, New Jersey, 1932. 24,289 gross tons; 705 feet long; 86 feet wide. Steam turbines, twin screw. Service speed 20 knots. 1,239 passengers as built (582 cabin class, 461 tourist class, 196 third class).]

ZAANDAM. This superb vessel is seen here (*above*) arriving in New York on her maiden voyage. The *Zaandam*'s high-standard, all-first-class quarters were designed, along with those of her sister ship *Noordam*, for the Rotterdam–New York service. Direct sailings took nine days. The *Zaandam* was used by the Americans as a troop transport beginning in 1942 and was torpedoed by a Nazi U-boat in the South Atlantic while on a voyage from East Africa to New York. Of 138 passengers and crew, only three survived— and only after enduring eighty-two days in a lifeboat. Rescued by a Brazilian patrol craft, their endurance in a lifeboat against the elements is the greatest record of its kind. [Built by Wilton-Fijenoord Shipyard, Rotterdam, Holland, 1939. 10,909 gross tons; 501 feet long; 64 feet wide. Burmeister & Wain diesels, twin screw. Service speed 17 knots. 148 all-first-class passengers.]

VICEROY OF INDIA. When completed in February 1929 for the London-Bombay, via Suez, service, the *Viceroy of India* was the pride of Britain's historic P&O Steam Navigation Company Limited. She was a single ship, without a sister, and established a separate identity. She sailed on many cruises to the Mediterranean, as well as northern Europe and Scandinavia. While serving as an Allied troopship, she was torpedoed on November 11, 1942, by a Nazi U-boat off Algiers and later sank (*below*). Having already disembarked her troops, she averted what might have been a major tragedy; only four perished. [Built by Alexander Stephen & Sons Limited, Glasgow, Scotland, 1929. 19,648 gross tons; 612 feet long; 76 feet wide. Turbo-electric engines, twin screw. Service speed 19 knots. 673 passengers (415 first class, 258 second class).]

REX. Mussolini's great liner fleet was in ruins as the war was changing course between 1943 and 1944. An ultimate Allied victory was becoming more and more apparent, and among the Axis victims was the pride and flagship of the Italian fleet, the splendid *Rex.* Completed in September 1932 she was the flagship of the newly amalgamated Italian Line, a combination of three of Italy's finest shipping companies, and sailed on the prestigious Naples–Genoa–New York run. She was not only the largest liner yet built and owned by the Italians, but the world's fastest ship for two years from 1933 to 1935. She is seen here (*above*) departing from New York's Pier 92 in February 1940. According to Steven Winograd, "The *Rex* was exciting! That was the best word to describe her. She represented the purposes and hopes of a nation. She was the great statement of Italian Fascism. She was also the traditional and conservative lady, but dressed in a risqué gown. She was the calmer of the two big Italian super liners of the 1930s, but certainly the more famous." Frank Trumbour added, "The *Rex* had a handsome exterior, and a flawless interior that bespoke Italian warmth and old-world tradition. Both her public and private rooms were sumptuous. Her lido was a masterpiece of outdoor glamour that established that wonderful trend for Italian liners ever after."

The *Rex* was used for normal commercial service as late as June 1940. She was then laid up, with rumors of being used by Mussolini ministers for trooping, or even conversion to an aircraft carrier. Nothing came to pass, and instead she was shifted from her homeport of Genoa to Bari, on the more secure Adriatic, and later near Trieste *(above)*. Left there in a quiet anchorage, she was a target for Allied aircraft and, even after the collapse of Mussolini's regime, she was bombed out, set afire, and then capsized in shallow water on September 8, 1944 *(opposite, top and bottom)*.

By the end of World War II in the summer of 1945, the Italian Line was in ruins. The *Rex* was finished, lying capsized on her port side at Capodistria, in the Gulf of Muggia, south of Trieste. Inevitably, there were studies made between 1945 and 1946 of possibly salvaging the liner, but she was beyond economic repair. She was declared a complete loss, with actual scrapping beginning in 1947, but not completed until 1958. [Built by Ansaldo Shipyard, Genoa, Italy, 1932. 51,062 gross tons; 880 feet long; 96 feet wide. Steam turbines, quadruple screw. Service speed 28 knots. 2,358 passengers (604 first class, 378 second class, 410 tourist class, 966 third class).]

CONTE DI SAVOIA. Like the *Rex*, the *Conte di Savoia* was senselessly destroyed and became another huge loss to the Italian fleet. The *Conte di Savoia* was the second largest Italian liner of the 1930s, but no less important than her running mate, the *Rex*. Many found the *Conte di Savoia* to be better looking, as well as the better decorated of the two. She is seen here *(above)* at Genoa. Steven Winograd reported, "She was one of my favorite liners of all time. She had great looks. She had two raked funnels that were placed far forward, yet she never seemed to be missing a third. This made her appear racy. Her interiors were, of course, over the top. She was glittering, vaulted, all chromium and glass, and never ceased to surprise even down in tourist class. She was so modern, an Art Deco explosion! She did not quite have the excitement of the *Rex*, but she had great style and, of course, had the first stabilizers on a big Atlantic liner." Frank Trumbour added, "The *Conte di Savoia*'s exterior lines were more solid looking, and perhaps more classic looking, than those of her more famous sister, the *Rex*. But her interiors did not have that warm, old-world look as did the *Rex*. Generally, much of the *Conte di Savoia*'s interior was sleek Deco in style. She was perhaps the beginning of the modern interior look that would follow after World War II on all Italian liners."

She too ran commercial sailings into the spring of 1940 well after war had started in northern Europe. Again, there were rumors that she would be used for trooping or be converted to an aircraft carrier, but these ideas were abandoned. She was moved to the Adriatic, to a quiet anchorage near Venice, and repainted in camouflage disguise *(below)*. But disaster ended her days. On September 11, 1943, the Nazi forces occupying northern Italy ordered that the ship be deliberately set afire to avoid capture or, worse still, escape to Allied waters. She burned out from end to end and then sank in shallow waters, an ending much like her former running mate, the slightly larger and faster *Rex*. The scorched hull of the *Conte di Savoia* was raised in October 1945 and there was some thought of rebuilding for Italian Line immigrant service, with 2,500 all-third-class berths, to run between Naples, Genoa, and the east coast of South America. Preliminary designs showed her having a single funnel. Also, both the Holland America Line and the French Line considered buying her for rebuilding as a companion to their *Nieuw Amsterdam* and *Liberté*, but neither plan came to pass. The laid-up hull was finally scrapped at Monfalcone between 1950 and 1951. [Built by Cantieri Riuniti dell'Adriatico, Monfalcone, Italy, 1932. 48,502 gross tons; 814 feet long; 96 feet wide. Steam turbines, quadruple screw. Service speed 27 knots. 2,200 passengers (500 first class, 366 second class, 412 tourist class, 922 third class).]

ASAMA MARU. "There are two notations regarding the *Asama Maru*, the eldest of three sisters designed to run the transpacific express service of the NYK Line," noted Hisashi Noma, Japan's foremost maritime historian and author. "On September 2, 1937, she encountered a big typhoon while undergoing a special survey at the Taikoo dockyard in Hong Kong. Pushed by the drifting Italian liner *Conte Verde*, the *Asama Maru* was tossed ashore in Saiwan Bay on the northeast coast of Hong Kong Island. After 3,500 tons of materials, including the main engines had been removed, she was finally refloated in March 1938 *(above)*. During the war she was used as a navy transport. On November 1, 1944, while cruising the Bashi Strait on a voyage from Manila to Japan, the *Asama Maru* was torpedoed by the U.S. submarine *Atule* and sank with the loss of 474 souls." [Built by Mitsubishi Shipbuilding & Engineering Company, Nagasaki, Japan, 1929. 16,975 gross tons; 583 feet long; 71 feet wide. Sulzer diesels, twin screw. Service speed 19 knots. 822 passengers (222 first class, 96 second class, 504 third class).]

WILHELM GUSTLOFF. Her tragic sinking, just months before the war officially ended, ranks as the worst maritime disaster of all time. Historically, she was also the first large cruise ship to be built and named by no less than Adolf Hitler. She was the first new build for the German Labor Front's (an arm of the Nazi Party) "Strength Through Joy" leisure agency. The purpose: to give less affluent members of the German community the opportunity of going on a cruise. It was to be a great hint of a Nazi-dominated world. And with the passengers and crew having equal accommodations, it was a preview of the social equality of the Nazi state. According to Hans Jurgen Witthoft, "She had only outside cabins, all of them cozily furnished and provided with hot and cold running water, and the crew were provided with exactly the same standard of comfort as the passengers. The *Wilhelm Gustloff* was definitely a special class of passenger vessel. According to a statement made by Blohm & Voss after the war, the German Labor Front aimed to build a large number of sister ships at Blohm & Voss—two vessels every year over ten years, which sounded somewhat unrealistic. The plan is said to have been submitted by Dr. Robert Ley, the head of the German Labor Front, to Adolf Hitler, who rejected the idea and ordered that warship construction was to have priority." Near sisters, the *Wilhelm Gustloff* is on the left and the *Robert Ley* on the right in this view *(below)* in Hamburg harbor from 1939.

Seen here departing from Hamburg (*above*), the *Wilhelm Gustloff* boasted very modern and comfortable interiors, while its amenities included a well-lighted indoor pool (*below*). Used from November 1940 as a moored accommodation ship in occupied Gdynia, the *Wilhelm Gustloff* was prepared for urgent evacuation service from the East by the end of 1944. According to German maritime expert and author Arnold Kludas, "She left Gotenhafen [Gdynia] on January 30 [1945] with 6,100 people onboard, mainly refugees and wounded. At 9:06 P.M., near Stolpmunde, the ship was hit by three torpedoes from the Soviet submarine *S-13* and began to sink. The heavy cruiser *Admiral Hipper*, which herself had 1,500 refugees onboard, arrived on the scene within a few minutes. Because of the still-present submarine danger, the cruiser broke off the rescue action that had begun. At 11:18 P.M., the *Wilhelm Gustloff* capsized and sank forty minutes later. German naval units and the North German Lloyd steamer *Gottingen*, which had been alerted by radio, were able to rescue only 904 survivors from the icy water. Approximately 5,200 perished." [Built by Blohm & Voss Shipbuilders, Hamburg, Germany, 1938. 25,484 gross tons; 684 feet long; 77 feet wide. MAN diesels, twin screw. Service speed 15.5 knots. 1,465 all-tourist-class passengers.]

CAP ARCONA. A fine, very popular liner on the Europe–South America run and the pride of the Hamburg–South America Line fleet, the *Cap Arcona* is unfortunately also remembered as a ship associated with enormous loss of life.

Built by Blohm & Voss at Hamburg, the 27,600-ton *Cap Arcona* was the finest of all the Hamburg–South America Line ships and, in fact, one of the very best ever to sail the South American route. Based on the earlier *Cap Polonio*, this grand three-stacker was commissioned in November 1927 and is seen here *(above)* in Hamburg harbor. At twenty knots, she made the run from Hamburg to Buenos Aires in just over two weeks. Beloved at her homeport of Hamburg, she was often called "the most wonderful ship in the German Merchant Navy."

Unfortunately, this 676-footer met with a horrific end. Like the *Wilhelm Gustloff* and other ships, she was used as an accommodation ship at Gdynia from November 1940. She was returned to sea in the winter of 1945 and made three voyages home to Germany, transporting 26,000 evacuees from the Nazi-occupied eastern territories. According to Arnold Kludas, "In April 1945 five thousand prisoners from the Neuengamme concentration camp were embarked while the ship was in the Bay of Lubeck. There were now 6,000 aboard, including the crew and guards. On May 3, the *Cap Arcona* was attacked by British fighter-bombers and set afire. Rockets and machine-gun fire from the aircraft destroyed almost all means of rescue. Panic broke out onboard, and shortly afterwards the *Cap Arcona* capsized. Although the ship was lying only a few hundred yards from shore, with a third of her width still out of the water, the disaster claimed 5,000 lives. The death of thousands of concentration camp prisoners was all the more tragic since it came at the hands of those who would have liberated them only a few days later. The wreck was broken up on the spot after the war. [Built by Blohm & Voss Shipbuilders, Hamburg, Germany, 1927. 27,560 gross tons; 676 feet long; 84 feet wide. Steam turbines, twin screw. Service speed 20 knots. 1,315 passengers (575 first class, 275 second class, 465 third class).]

JOHN ERICSSON. While she might have been destroyed totally during a fire at her New York pier, she went on to sail in further service with great success. Built as the very popular *Kungsholm*, the flagship of the Swedish American Line, she sailed in both North Atlantic service to New York as well as on luxury cruises until sold in January 1942, to the U.S. government for wartime trooping. She is seen here *(above)* departing from New York's Pier 97 on September 16, 1939, wearing "neutrality markings" along her sides for an otherwise regular sailing to Copenhagen and Gothenburg. Renamed USS *John Ericsson*, she continued in postwar repatriation and war bride service until March 1947, when she burned at Pier 90 at the foot of West 50th Street in New York. It might have been an even greater tragedy if the fire had spread to the pier itself and to the giant *Queen Elizabeth*, berthed on the other side. Sold back to the Swedish American Line and then to their affiliate, the newly formed Home Lines, she was repaired as the *Italia*. Used in transatlantic and cruise service until 1964, she then became the *Imperial Bahama Hotel*, a floating hotel at Freeport on Grand Bahama Island, but with little success. Within a year, she was sold to Spanish ship breakers and towed across the Atlantic to Bilbao for demolition. [Built by Blohm & Voss Shipbuilders, Hamburg, Germany, 1928. 20,223 gross tons; 609 feet long; 78 feet wide. Burmeister & Wain diesels, twin screw. Service speed 17 knots. 1,575 passengers as built (115 first class, 490 second class, 970 third class).]

GEORGE WASHINGTON. Built in 1909 for North German Lloyd, this 25,500-tonner was one of the largest ships of her day and followed the German tendency of the time to use American names in an effort to recruit more of the westbound European immigrant trade. It was widely believed that arriving onboard a ship with such a name eased entry procedures, especially at Ellis Island in New York harbor. Left at Lloyd's Hoboken terminal when World War I started in the summer of 1914, the *George Washington* was later seized by the U.S. government, used as an Allied trooper, and then sailed in peacetime service, from New York to Bremerhaven, for the United States Lines. An aging victim of the Depression, "Big George," as she was dubbed, was laid up for most of the 1930s. She was briefly restored for military service in 1940 as the renamed *Catlin,* but then reverted to *George Washington.* She is seen here (*above*) at the Philadelphia Naval Shipyard on March 17, 1941, being prepared for military service. The *George Washington* was damaged in a New York pier fire in 1947 and then again in a blaze at Baltimore three years later (*below*). By then, she was far too old to be repaired and so went to local breakers. [Built by A. G. Vulcan Shipyard, Stettin, Germany, 1908. 23,788 gross tons; 722 feet long; 78 feet wide. Steam quadruple-expansion engines, twin screw. Service speed 18.5 knots. 6,500 troops during World War II.]

MONARCH OF BERMUDA. "After the *Monarch of Bermuda* burned at Newcastle on March 24, 1947, there was a plan to make her hull into an aircraft carrier," said naval architect James Wheeler. "She had burned for several days and was just a hulk in the end. Furness-Bermuda Line lost interest in her and she was declared a total loss. She was just a bit of rubbish really. But it was decided to rebuild her for the pressing Australian immigrant trade. It would cost $1 million—half to be paid by the British government and half by the Australian government." The *Monarch of Bermuda* had been one of the grandest 1930s ocean liners. Completed in December 1931, the three-stacker, designed to resemble the big Atlantic liners, was created for the cruise service between New York and Bermuda, a six-day round-trip then costing $50.00 and up. She is seen here (*above*) in a view dated October 9, 1931, being fitted out at Newcastle-upon-Tyne. She was owned by the Furness-Bermuda Line and was joined, in 1933, by a close sister, the *Queen of Bermuda*. She became an Allied trooper in November 1939 and served with the British government for almost eight years. She was to be restored for Bermuda sailings when she caught fire.

Renamed *New Australia* and with a capacity of 1,693 all-one-class passengers, the rebuilt former *Monarch of Bermuda* was managed for the British Ministry of Transport by the Shaw Savill Line.

Her only purpose: to carry low-fare immigrants on the run from Southampton to Fremantle, Melbourne, and Sydney via Port Said and Aden. She had been a splendid, three-funnel luxury liner, but was now far from a pretty ship. Only a middle funnel remained, assisted by a bipod mast that acted as a second exhaust. She was long and flat with cluttered upper decks. All the public rooms were on one deck.

"She was a 'utility ship,'" added Wheeler. "The *New Australia* was so basic. She was painted white from end to end with sprayed cork on the ceilings. She had the thickest linoleum floors. The Greek Line bought her in 1958 and converted her at Blohm & Voss in Hamburg. She had a dead-straight bow that the Greek Line modified. Her main purpose was to provide mostly tourist-class service to and from eastern Canada and north European ports. She did provide some first-class quarters, which were done in very modern German style. All of their cabins had private facilities and were located on the upper deck along the starboard side. There was a small restaurant and a bar lounge. We carried lots of officers of the Canadian Armed Forces then stationed in West Germany. Tourist class had lots of six- and eight-berth cabins without washbasins. These were actually quite out-of-date by the late '50s. Later, we added basins."

The Greek Line found the *Arkadia (opposite, bottom)* to be a very successful ship. "Once, I remember that Mr. Chandris [Chandris Lines] called Mr. Goulandris [Greek Line] for help," said Wheeler. "Chandris needed to replace his *Brittany* for one voyage and so the *Arkadia* made one nostalgic voyage out to Australia from Southampton. She was full up on the homeward sailing, Goulandris made a packet and then returned empty. Mr. Goulandris actually thought of entering the Australian trade and later actually discussed joint Chandris-Goulandris services, including a transatlantic business as well. Otherwise, the *Arkadia* spent her winters on very popular two-week cruises to the Canaries and Madeira, sailing from Tilbury and Southampton. She was so suc- cessful, *Lakonia* was bought to join her, but on a year-round basis."

The Atlantic service to Canada declined steadily in the early '60s. Sailings on the *Arkadia* were reduced and sometimes includ- ed added ports to increase passenger loads. She was simply too old to be converted for year-round cruising, and so in November 1966 she was sold to Spanish breakers. She was demolished at Valencia and at just about the same time as her long ago, near-sister, the *Queen of Bermuda*, was meeting her end up in Scotland. [Built by Vickers-Armstrong Shipbuilders Limited, Newcastle-upon-Tyne, England, 1931. 22,424 gross tons; 579 feet long; 76 feet wide. Steam turbo-electric engines, quadruple screw. Service speed 19 knots. 830 passengers (799 first class, 31 second class).]

MAGDALENA. Designed to revive the postwar South American liner services of Britain's Royal Mail Lines and be a companion to the well-known *Andes* and *Alcantara*, the sleek-looking *Magdalena (above)* was a most unfortunate ship. "On her homeward maiden voyage from Buenos Aires to London, the *Magdalena* ran onto the Tijucas rocks off Rio de Janeiro, on April 25 [1949]," according to Arnold Kludas. "The passengers and part of the crew were taken off. On the twenty-sixth, the ship was refloated. But during the voyage under tow to Rio de Janeiro, off Fort Sao Joao, the forepart broke off just forward of the superstructure and sank. The rest of the hull was stranded in Imbui Bay and was sold in June to a Brazilian firm for breaking up." [Built by Harland & Wolff Limited, Belfast, Northern Ireland, 1949. 17,547 gross tons; 570 feet long; 73 feet wide. Steam turbines, twin screw. Service speed 18 knots. 479 passengers (133 first class, 346 third class).]

CHAMPOLLION. Built as a three-funnel passenger ship for France's Messageries Maritimes, the *Champollion* was rebuilt and modernized with a single funnel in 1950, following her war service as a troopship *(above)*. Resuming eastern Mediterranean service, she was wrecked while approaching Beirut in bad weather on December 22, 1952. Stranded on a reef south of the harbor entrance, the *Champollion* sat just 600 feet from a nearby beach. She began to list seriously and then cracked in two just aft of the funnel. However, thanks to the exceptional efforts of the Beirut pilots and their crews, all but fifteen onboard the stricken liner were rescued. The wreck of the *Champollion* was later sold to local Lebanese scrappers. [Built by Constructions Navales, La Ciotat, France, 1925. 12,546 gross tons; 550 feet long; 62 feet wide. Steam triple-expansion engines, twin screw. Service speed 17.5 knots. 499 passengers (207 first class, 142 second class, 150 third class).]

KLIPFONTEIN. "The Dutch and some Germans used the rounded Maierform bow because, so they believed, it reduced resistance at sea. In the end, however, I do not think it was very successful," commented the late Everett Viez. Several passenger ships including the *Klipfontein (below)* of the Holland-Africa Line had Maierform bows. "The *Klipfontein*, named after a place in South Africa, was, on January 8, 1953, at 1:15 in the afternoon, traveling from Maputo to Beira, when she ran afoul of an underwater rock," noted Dr. Nico Guns. "All passengers and crew boarded the lifeboats. The British liner *Bloemfontein Castle* rescued all of them. But three hours later, the *Klipfontein* sank over the bow towards the deep." [Built by P. Smit, Jr., Rotterdam, Holland, 1939. 10,544 gross tons; 520 feet long; 63 feet wide. Burmeister & Wain diesels, twin screw. Service speed 17 knots. 148 passengers (106 first class, 42 tourist class).]

EMPRESS OF CANADA. Because of the Coronation of Queen Elizabeth II in London in June 1953, Canadian Pacific Steamships was—like all North Atlantic liner companies—heavily booked. So, the loss of one of their liners could not have come at a less opportune time. "It was fortunate that, after the war, Canadian Pacific had two surviving Duchess ships to reactivate. Splendid ships, they were medium-sized and so ideal for the resumption of the St. Lawrence trade," said Everett Viez. "Refitted, they were comfortable, restyled to two classes and looked very smart in their white hulls topped off by the yellow funnels and the postwar Canadian Pacific checkers."

Used on the run to Quebec City and Montreal, the *Empress of Canada (above)*, built originally as the *Duchess of Richmond* and renamed between 1946 and 1947, caught fire at Liverpool on January 25, 1953. Overloaded with firefighters' water, she capsized against the pier itself and was badly damaged *(below)*. Beyond repair, she was salvaged, sold to Italian scrappers and broken up at La Spezia in 1954. [Built by John Brown & Company Limited, Clydebank, Scotland, 1928. 20,325 gross tons; 600 feet long; 75 feet wide. Steam turbines, twin screw. Service speed 18 knots. 700 passengers (397 first class, 303 tourist class).]

EMPIRE WINDRUSH. Several pre–World War II German liners passed into Allied hands beginning in 1945. Some went to the British, others to the Soviets, and at least one to the Americans. Hamburg–South America Line's *Monte Rosa*, a sister to the aforementioned *Monte Cervantes*, found further life as the British Ministry of Transport's peacetime trooper *Empire Windrush* (*above*).

She was almost lost at the very end of the war. According to Arnold Kludas, "On February 16, 1945, off Hela [in the Baltic], the *Monte Rosa* struck a mine and was damaged aft. Listing, with a flooded engine room, the ship was towed to Gotenhafen [Gdynia]. She was temporarily repaired with materials available onboard and then towed to Copenhagen, carrying over 5,000 wounded and refugees. She was taken to Kiel in May and seized as a prize of war." Repaired and refitted, the British government's Ministry of Transport began using her in 1946 as the all-white *Empire Windrush*. She ran peacetime military sailings. During a voyage with troops from Yokohama to Southampton, she caught fire following an explosion in her engine room while in the western Mediterranean on March 28, 1954. The ship was abandoned; all but four of those aboard were rescued. The British warship *Saintes* tried to tow the burning ship to Gibraltar, but it sank on the twenty-ninth. [Built by Blohm & Voss Shipbuilders, Hamburg, Germany, 1931. 14,651 gross tons; 524 feet long; 66 feet wide. MAN diesels, twin screw. Service speed 14.5 knots. Approximately 1,500 passengers and troops by 1946.]

ANDREA DORIA. It was the first major maritime disaster involving a well-known Atlantic liner that was brought into American homes via black-and-white television. The late Everett Viez once told me, "The *Andrea Doria* was one of the finest and loveliest liners of her day, and so her sinking was a great loss. But she had developed steering problems, we heard, at the beginning of that July 1956 westbound crossing to New York. The captain had asked to postpone the voyage and go to dry dock, but since it was the height of the summer season, the Italian Line's Genoa offices refused. The ship was heavily booked and so was the *Saturnia* that followed her to New York. The Italian Line did not want to lose or disappoint passengers. And, of course, the *Andrea Doria* had stability problems from the very beginning. The combination of steering and stability problems proved to be decisive factors in the collision and her sinking. In fact, after the collision she should have begun sinking in an upright position, not listing immediately to starboard. It is believed that the Italian Line was aware of this and, among other decisions, reportedly paid for the repairs to the *Stockholm*, which, of course, rammed the *Andrea Doria*. Furthermore, all the Swedish American Line officers continued with their seagoing careers and often were promoted. The Italian officers, on the other hand, seemed to vanish into obscurity. In fact, the captain of the *Andrea Doria* suffered emotional collapse from which he never recovered."

Steven Winograd added, "The *Andrea Doria* is immortalized, but there was more hype over her demise than the ship itself. Her sister, the *Cristoforo Colombo*, actually had far better decor. The *Andrea Doria* was, of course, the first new Italian liner since the *Rex* of 1932 and was the hope and breath of postwar Italy. She was very beautiful on the outside, but actually quite disappointing on the inside. The *Cristoforo Colombo* had much more carpeting and a better feel within." New York harbor historian and photographer Fred Rodriguez added, "Watching the *Andrea Doria* sink before my eyes on the old black-and-white television was mesmerizing. I was eight years old at the time and it actually prompted my lifelong interest in ships." The *Andrea Doria* is seen here (*opposite*) in a classic gathering of liners along New York's Luxury Liner Row. Shown in February 1956 from top to bottom: the *Empress of Scotland*, Canadian Pacific Steamships; the *Franconia*, *Mauretania*, *Queen Mary*, and *Caronia*, all Cunard; the *Ile de France*, French Line; the *America*, United States Lines; the *Andrea Doria*, Italian Line; and the *Constitution*, American Export Lines.

Clear skies with warm sunshine gave way to a foggy night on July 25, 1956, the day before the *Andrea Doria* was due in New York. She was on a regular westbound crossing, steaming at twenty-one knots on her usual routing from Naples, Genoa, Cannes, and Gibraltar. Among the 1,708 passengers and crew aboard, the first-class passenger list included Hollywood actress Ruth Roman, several minor American politicians, a pair of European ballet dancers and the mayor of Philadelphia. With the evening fog, her captain began to worry that he might have to reduce speed and therefore delay her arrival at Pier 84, closely scheduled by the home office for eight the next morning. That same day, the Swedish American liner *Stockholm* had left Pier 97, thirteen New York City streets north of the Italian Line terminal, at eleven o'clock in the morning on an eastbound crossing to Copenhagen and Gothenburg. Thirty minutes later, from Pier 88, at West 48th Street, French Line's *Ile de France* cast off, also on an eastward passage, to Plymouth and Le Havre. All three ships would have, quite unexpectedly, a fateful meeting later that night.

At eleven P.M., in thickening fog off Nantucket, the officers aboard the *Andrea Doria* noticed the lights of another ship. Radar had not yet been perfected and the first blip of that other ship was miscalculated and quickly came much closer. She was believed to be a small freighter. In fact, it was the *Stockholm* and the two liners were traveling at a combined speed of forty knots or forty-six miles per hour and therefore moving at the rate of approximately one mile per minute. At 11:21 P.M., the *Stockholm* rammed the *Andrea Doria*, which abruptly and dramatically lurched over to port and then righted. Passengers and crew heard the sounds of a grinding crash, and some saw the bright lights of the *Stockholm* through the *Andrea Doria's* windows and portholes. The Swedish ship's reinforced bow was like a dagger piercing the larger Italian. She cut forty feet into the *Andrea Doria's* hull, just below the bridge, creating a jagged hole like an inverted pyramid that extended from below the waterline up to B deck. It was a mortal wound. The two liners remained impaled for a short time until movement tore them free, and fifty-five feet of the *Stockholm's* foredeck and bow were folded into a tangled mass of steel. The *Andrea Doria* sent out an immediate SOS and began the starboard list from which she would never recover. With her fuel tanks empty, she had very little ballast. The ships were some forty-five miles south of Nantucket Island, a sea-lane known as the "Crossroads of the Atlantic" because of its busy shipping pattern. No less than eleven U.S. Coast Guard cutters were immediately dispatched to sea following the first calls for help from the stricken *Andrea Doria*.

It was soon realized that although badly damaged, the *Stockholm* was in no danger of sinking and so she began to assist with the rescue of the *Andrea Doria*. Below decks on the Italian ship, crewmen struggled quickly and furiously to pump out the floods of invading Atlantic water. Deck crews worked promptly to rig rope ladders and nets so passengers could climb down the ship's sides and reach waiting lifeboats. While all the port side lifeboats were useless because of the severe, ever-increasing list to starboard, the *Andrea Doria's* electrical system still operated, and was greatly helped by huge boat deck emergency searchlights.

Passengers slid down ropes—off the stern, off the bow, off the quarter deck. Small children and the elderly were carried. The steady relay of lifeboats throughout the night, while largely successful, was at times a clumsy affair. The boats were often unwieldy and were manned by cooks, waiters, and even bellhops. The *Andrea Doria's* whistle moaned continuously—her own death rattle. A small armada of ships began to gather around the liner as passengers and crew alike fled to safety. For a time, radio traffic between the rescue ships and the shore became overloaded and confusing. By daylight, the *Andrea Doria* was heeled over and abandoned (*left, first three photos*). The last of the passengers were removed by five o'clock, over four hours after the collision. Only Captain Calamai and a few officers remained onboard, hoping that the stricken liner might somehow be saved. Below, the pumps still throbbed as tons of seawater were pumped overboard to no avail. By daybreak, it was apparent there was no hope. The captain and his last remaining crew members were taken off the sinking liner. The U.S. Coast Guard cutter *Evergreen* flashed the official obituary to the world: "SS *Andrea Doria* sank in 225 feet of water at 10:09 A.M." The cutter marked the grave with a floating tombstone—a yellow buoy. There were 1,662 saved, but fifty-two were lost (forty-six from the *Andrea Doria* and six from the *Stockholm*). Now, the ships that had kept the deathwatch got underway. The stern of the *Ile de France*, lined with passengers and survivors, is seen here (*left, bottom*) as the great French liner nears New York.

Extensive, very confidential inquiries and hearings followed the tragedy. Final compensation amounted to $48 million, but no precise responsibility was determined. The final investigation and findings were dropped by the mutual consent of both the Italian Line and the Swedish American Line. The disaster did lead, however, to greatly increased radar navigation training for ships' officers. The *Stockholm*, with a badly damaged bow, is seen here *(above)* as repairs commenced in a Brooklyn shipyard.

By 2006, fifty years after her sinking, the wreckage of the *Andrea Doria* was deteriorating at increasing speed, possibly due to the global warming of the seawater. Her funnel and upper decks are gone, disintegrated down to the promenade deck area. Moreover, some forty divers have been lost in their attempts to dive on the sunken liner. [Built by Ansaldo Shipyards, Genoa, Italy, 1952, 29,083 gross tons; 700 feet long; 90 feet wide. Steam turbines, twin screw. Service speed 23 knots. 1,241 passengers (218 first class, 320 cabin class, 703 tourist class).]

HILDEBRAND. Britain's Booth Line ran a rather interesting passenger service sailing from Liverpool and then across the southern Atlantic to Brazil and traveling 1,000 miles up the mighty Amazon River to Manaus. The *Hildebrand*, a passenger-cargo ship *(above)*, was their ship of postwar revival. On September 25, 1957, outbound from Liverpool, she stranded in heavy fog off Cascais, near Lisbon. Unable to be refloated, she was abandoned as a complete loss. [Built by Cammell, Laird & Company Limited, Birkenhead, England, 1951. 7,735 gross tons; 421 feet long; 60 feet wide. Steam turbines, single screw. Service speed 15 knots. 170 passengers (74 first class, 96 tourist class).]

NEPTUNIA. After World War II, older ships often found further life in low-fare tourist and immigrant services. The Greek Line invested in this market, running services to the U.S. and eastern Canada from both the Mediterranean and northern Europe. Among their vintage ships was the former Dutch *Johan de Witt*, completed in 1920, but sailing as the Greek *Neptunia* in the 1950s. She is seen here *(below)* at Boston. Used on the North Atlantic run, between Bremerhaven, other ports, and New York, she rammed Daunt's Rock, near Cobh in Ireland, on November 2, 1957, and was later beached. The damages were so serious that, in view of her thirty-seven years of service, she was abandoned to the underwriters. Later sealed, the *Neptunia* was towed to Rotterdam for scrapping. [Built by Netherlands Shipbuilding Company, Amsterdam, Holland, 1920. 10,519 gross tons; 523 feet long; 59 feet wide. Steam triple-expansion engines, twin screw. Service speed 15 knots. 787 passengers (39 first class, 748 tourist class).]

SKAUBRYN. Another method of serving the low-fare tourist and immigrant markets following World War II was to convert cargo ships into passenger ships. Actually intended to be a freighter, the *Skaubryn* was converted for the booming Europe-Australia passenger trade. She is shown (*above*) arriving in Sydney harbor. But on March 31, 1958, during a voyage between Bremerhaven and Sydney, this otherwise small passenger ship caught fire while in the Indian Ocean. A nearby British freighter, the *City of Sydney*, rescued all 1,300 passengers and crew, but the charred hulk itself could not withstand rescue. It sank while under tow on April 6. [Built by Gotaverken Shipyard, Gothenburg, Sweden, 1951. 9,786 gross tons; 458 feet long; 57 feet wide. Diesels, twin screw. Service speed 16.5 knots. 1,221 passengers (16 first class, 1,205 tourist class).]

TARSUS. She was the flagship of the Turkish Merchant Marine, the largest ship of her day in the Turkish Maritime Lines fleet. In the 1950s, she made several transatlantic crossings between Istanbul, other Mediterranean ports, and New York. She is seen here (*below*) at Pier 88. "She was a lovely ship, which retained much of her prewar style and ambience in her postwar, Turkish days. It was a treat to visit her in 1960, when she made some New York–Bermuda cruises for a short-lived operation called Fiesta Cruise Lines," noted Captain James McNamara. Built as American Export Lines' *Exochorda* for New York–Mediterranean sailings, she served in World War II as the USS *Harry Lee* before being sold to Turkey in 1946. Her end came on December 14, 1960, when, after two tankers collided and then caught fire in Istanbul harbor, one of the burning ships drifted, slammed into the *Tarsus* and set her afire. The passenger ship was completely destroyed. [Built by New York Shipbuilding Company, Camden, New Jersey, 1931. 9,451 gross tons; 475 feet long; 62 feet wide. Steam turbines, single screw. Service speed 15 knots. 465 passengers from 1946 (189 first class, 66 second class, 210 third class).]

ALCOA CORSAIR. Over 500 Victory ships were built during World War II. Suitable as freighters with five hatches for cargo, and as much as sixteen- to seventeen-knot service speeds, they were designed not only to assist in wartime service, but to revitalize commercial services once the hostilities ended. Several were found suitable for conversion to passenger ships. New York–based Alcoa Steamship Company had three converted Victory ships for their New Orleans–Caribbean services: the *Alcoa Cavalier, Alcoa Clipper,* and *Alcoa Corsair.* They were given high-standard, all-first-class accommodations. By 1960, their services fading, they had become money losers for their owners. Ironically, on her last voyage, the *Alcoa Corsair* collided in the lower Mississippi River with the Italian freighter *Lorenzo Marcello.* The *Corsair* was left with a 150-foot-long gash along her starboard side *(above).* Five passengers and five crew died. Flooding and beginning to sink, the ship was sensibly beached. Rebuilt as a tramp freighter, she was broken up in Japan in 1963. [Built by Oregon Shipbuilding Corporation, Portland, Oregon, 1947. 8,481 gross tons; 455 feet long; 62 feet wide. Steam turbines, single screw. Service speed 16.5 knots. 95 all-first-class passengers.]

DARA. Well into the 1960s Britain maintained a sizeable passenger fleet that never touched British shores. These ships were based in places such as Africa, the Middle East, Australia, and the Orient. Some of them, in third- and deck-class quarters, carried an Eastern version of steerage. The *Dara* was one of four sisters built for British India Line's Bombay–Persian Gulf local service *(below).* An otherwise unremarkable, smallish passenger vessel, she made international headlines when, on April 8, 1961, a terrorist bomb exploded and ignited a large fire onboard. In all, 238 passengers and crew perished. Abandoned, but later placed under tow, the *Dara* sank on April 10. [Built by Barclay Curle & Company Limited, Glasgow, Scotland, 1948. 5,030 gross tons; 399 feet long; 65 feet wide. Doxford diesel, single screw. Service speed 14 knots. 1,028 passengers (13 first class, 65 second class, 950 deck class).]

BIANCA C. The *Bianca C* cruised from New York to the Caribbean in the winter of 1959 to 1960 with much attention. She was said to be one of the finest Italian liners of her day with modern interiors, fine food and service, and well-known Italian ambience. "She and the little *Franca C* were two of the very first Costa liners to cruise from the United States and impress the traveling public with the Italians' high ability to make older ships appear far more contemporary, almost new," said Everett Viez. Certainly, the *Bianca C* appeared almost to be a new ship, but was, in fact, laid down in 1939 for Messageries Maritimes and their Marseilles–Far East services. Delayed by the war, she was launched in June 1944 as the *Marechal Petain*, but delayed again and finally completed in 1949 as the *La Marseillaise*. In 1957, she became the Swiss-owned transatlantic liner *Arosa Sky*, and then, in 1959, Costa's *Bianca C*. She is seen here *(above)* arriving in New York for the first time in May 1957. Used generally in Genoa–West Indies service, she too fell victim to a malady common to French-built liners: fire. She burned out completely off St. George, Grenada, in the eastern Caribbean, then heeled over and finally sank on October 24, 1961.

[Built by Constructions Navales, La Ciotat, France, 1939-44. 18,247 gross tons; 592 feet long; 75 feet wide. Sulzer diesels, triple screw. Service speed 20 knots. 1,230 passengers (200 first class, 1,030 tourist class).]

VENEZUELA. An older Italian liner, the *Venezuela* might have had a few more years of service had it not been for a mishap at Cannes on March 17, 1962. After stranding on local rocks with her passengers and crew being taken ashore, she was refloated four weeks later. But her age and the cost of repairs outweighed her return to service. She was sold to ship breakers at nearby La Spezia in Italy. The *Venezuela* had been the French Line's *De Grasse* (1920–53) and then sailed as the *Empress of Australia* for Canadian Pacific (1953–56). She joined Italy's Grimaldi-Siosa Lines in 1956 and became the *Venezuela*. She is seen here *(below)* at Lisbon. [Built by Cammell, Laird & Company, Birkenhead, England, 1924. 18,769 gross tons; 597 feet long; 71 feet wide. Steam turbines, twin screw. Service speed 18 knots. 1,480 passengers (180 first class, 500 cabin class, 800 tourist class).]

BRITTANY. The Greek Chandris Lines was set on becoming one of the biggest operators in the booming, highly lucrative Europe-Australia migrant and tourist trades of the 1960s. They began with the *Patris*, the former *Bloemfontein Castle* in 1959, and then soon looked for a second ship. She was the French *Bretagne*, which was later refitted as the *Brittany*. She is shown here (*above*) arriving in New York for the first time in June 1961. But her Greek days proved short. The *Bretagne*, built for the Marseilles–South America run of France's Transports Maritimes, joined Chandris in 1961, began sailing between Europe and Australia for most of the year and then, in 1962, was renamed *Brittany*. Her days were numbered, however. On April 8, 1963, while at the Skaramanga Shipyard near Piraeus, she burned from end to end in a fire started by a welder's torch. Burned out, sunk, and later declared a complete loss, she was salvaged, but only to be sold to Italian scrap merchants. She was broken up at La Spezia the following summer. [Built by Chantiers et Ateliers de St. Nazaire, St. Nazaire, France, 1952. 16,355 gross tons; 58l feet long; 73 feet wide. Steam turbines, twin screw. Service speed 19 knots. 1,200 passengers as *Brittany* (150 first class, 1,050 tourist class).]

LAKONIA. Here is the classic case of an elderly liner being pressed into further service, possibly well past her prime. According to Nico Guns, "When built, she was one of the finest Dutch passenger liners with magnificent decoration." Captain McNamara added, "In the early 1960s, when she was still sailing for the Dutch, she was a very interesting ship, a very dark ship on the inside and clearly an old ship, in fact a very old ship." Built for the Nederland Line's colonial service between Amsterdam and the Dutch East Indies via Suez, the *Johan van Oldenbarnevelt*, as she was dubbed, served as an Allied troopship and then returned to Dutch commercial liner service until sold in 1962. The Greek Line bought her for cruising from Southampton, England. Renamed *Lakonia*, she was on a festive, eleven-day Christmas cruise to the Canary Islands when she caught fire off Madeira on December 22, 1963 (*below*). Chaos among the 651 passengers followed. In the end, 128 people perished—ninety-five passengers and thirty-three crew. Placed under tow, the still burning, but empty *Lakonia* sank on December 29. [Built by Netherlands Shipbuilding Company, Amsterdam, Holland, 1930. 20,314 gross tons; 609 feet long; 75 feet wide. Sulzer diesels, twin screw. Service speed 16.5 knots. 1,210 one-class passengers.]

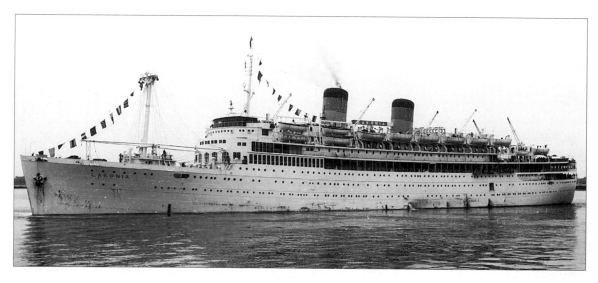

RIO DE LA PLATA. The *Rio de la Plata* and her two sisters, the *Rio Jachal* and *Rio Tunuyan*, were familiar sights along lower Manhattan's waterfront. They tended to arrive on Saturdays and then sail the following Friday from their Franklin Street berths on six-week round-trips to the east coast of South America. "The *Rio de la Plata* [**above**] and her two sisters were typical Italian-Ansaldo new builds. They were sleek, good-looking, well-proportioned, and great cargo ships blended with passenger accommodation," noted Captain James McNamara. Refitted for Buenos Aires–Hamburg sailings in 1963, the *Rio de la Plata* lasted but a year in this service before she was swept by fire on November 19, 1964. She was undergoing repairs at the time in a Buenos Aires shipyard. Her blackened hull was not scrapped until 1968. Her sister *Rio Jachal* burned out as well, at New York's Pier 25, in a nighttime blaze on September 28, 1962 [**below**]. She burned a second time, in 1968, before being broken up a year later. [Built by Ansaldo Shipyards, Genoa, Italy, 1951. 11,317 gross tons; 550 feet long; 66 feet wide. Fiat diesels, twin screw. Service speed 18.5 knots. 116 all-first-class passengers as built.]

YARMOUTH CASTLE. The tragic burning of this aged cruise ship made headlines and prompted investigations and hearings that called for much more stringent safety standards for passenger ships sailing from American ports. The little *Yarmouth Castle* (her twin sister the *Yarmouth* is pictured **above**) was rather typical of the many cruise ships sailing from U.S. ports in the 1950s and '60s. She was old, tired, and over-painted. Fred Rodriguez visited the ship at Pier 32 in New York during a summer season of cruises in 1965. "She really wasn't the perfect cruise ship. She had the smallest pool I've ever seen on a ship, for example, and it was located in the very stern of the ship with what seemed to be a two-foot-wide walkway around it. Inside, she had lots of dark woods, was very small, and very cramped in places."

Built for the American-flag Eastern Steamship Lines, the sisters *Evangeline* and *Yarmouth* were "mini ocean liners" and sailed between Boston and Nova Scotia in summer and between New York and the Caribbean in winter. Re-flagged to Liberian colors by 1954, the two ships became pioneer cruise ships, departing from the then infant port of Miami. In 1963, the *Evangeline* was sold by Eastern, then headquartered in Miami, to another local operator, Yarmouth Cruise Lines. Renamed *Yarmouth Castle*, she was running twice weekly, three- and four-day cruises between Miami and Nassau when, on November 13, 1965, she caught fire. It was close to one in the morning as the fire spread quickly and poor seamanship, confusion, and chaos followed. At the time, Captain Carl Netherland-Brown was master of the cruise ship *Bahama Star*, the principal rescue ship in the *Yarmouth Castle* fire. "Both were still good, sound ships, even in their later years. Their owners had spent considerable amounts on safety. We were both bound for Nassau when the fire occurred. Once alerted, we headed at top speed toward the flames. Our lifeboats were swung out and ready. It took only one trip to the burning *Yarmouth Castle* to collect all the survivors. But many were lost, never having left their cabins. In all, we rescued 375 passengers and 130 crew. The *Bahama Star* was as close as 200 feet from the *Yarmouth Castle* and we could feel the intense heat. We had to move further away." By six o'clock in the morning, the flaming hulk of the

Yarmouth Castle had slipped under the waves. [Built by William Cramp & Sons Shipbuilding & Engine Building Company, Philadelphia, Pennsylvania, 1927. 5,002 gross tons; 379 feet long; 56 feet wide. Steam turbines, twin screw. Service speed 18 knots. Approximately 350 cruise passengers.]

VIKING PRINCESS. Fire safety standards for passenger ships, especially older, often rebuilt, foreign ones, were officially heightened following the loss of this cruise liner. The late ocean liner historian and photographer Everett Viez told me, "The *Viking Princess* was a rather good rebuild, having been a passenger-cargo ship made over as a full-time cruise ship. But she was still very French in ways. The French, it seems by their many, many passenger-ship fires, have always had electrical problems, especially with the wiring and fittings behind the woodwork. It seems it has always been faulty." Fred Rodriguez added, "I visited her several times and thought she made a very good conversion. But by 1965, she was overshadowed by the brand-new, glittering, innovative *Oceanic*, completed the same year."

The *Viking Princess* was built as the combination passenger-cargo ship *Lavoisier* for Paris-based Compagnie Maritime des Chargeurs Reunis with 300 berths in first- and third-class quarters. She sailed between northern Europe and the east coast of South America until sold to Italian buyers in 1961 and rebuilt as the 600-bed cruise ship *Riviera Prima*. She is shown here (**opposite, top**), in a photo dated May 8, 1963, undergoing repairs at Bethlehem Steel's Key Highway Shipyard at Baltimore. Sold to Norwegian owners in October 1964 she was refitted as the *Viking Princess* and cruised under the banner of Viking Cruise Lines. During a Caribbean voyage, she caught fire off Cuba, on April 8, 1966, and was abandoned (**opposite, bottom**). Her charred remains were later towed to Spain for demolition. [Built by Ateliers et Chantiers de la Loire, St. Nazaire, France, 1950. 12,812 gross tons; 537 feet long; 64 feet wide. Sulzer diesels, twin screw. Service speed 16 knots. 600 cruise passengers.]

HANSEATIC. While fire is often damaging, it is sometimes the smell of smoke that dooms a ship, especially an older one. Quite simply, the smell cannot be removed. "The smell of smoke permeated the wood panels on older liners and, no matter how much cleansing and cleaning, it could not be eliminated," noted Captain James McNamara. "The *Hanseatic* was a great loss because she was a great ship. I remember her as the *Empress of Scotland*, with her three checkered funnels, and then, in great contrast, as the rebuilt, modernized *Hanseatic*. It was one of the great conversions of the 1950s."

Built as the *Empress of Japan* for Canadian Pacific's Vancouver–Far East service, she was renamed *Empress of Scotland* in 1942. She returned to commercial service, after war duties, on the company's Atlantic run between Liverpool and New York. A three-stacker, she was bought by the newly created Hamburg Atlantic Line in 1957, totally rebuilt with two funnels, and then recommissioned as the modernized *Hanseatic* in the summer of 1958 *(above)*. "I had my first shipboard meal, superb German cooking, onboard the *Hanseatic* at Pier 84 in New York and remember her as a very beautiful, good-looking ship," recalled Fred Rodriguez. "She had unique, oversized postcards that were actually playable records, renditions of the crew singing the *Hanseatic* theme song. I was due to visit her on September 7, 1966, but missed the opportunity, of course. She caught fire." *(opposite, top)* The sailing was canceled, and the ship taken to a nearby Brooklyn shipyard for inspection, but it turned out that repairs would be too costly given the ship's thirty-six years. She was towed to Hamburg that fall and scrapped locally *(opposite, bottom)*. [Built by Fairfield Shipbuilding & Engineering Company, Glasgow, Scotland, 1930. 30,029 gross tons; 672 feet long; 83 feet wide. Steam turbines, twin screw. Service speed 21 knots. 1,252 passengers (85 first class, 1,167 tourist class).]

HERAKLION. The loss of the *Heraklion* prompted the collapse of one of Greece's largest and fastest growing passenger lines of the 1960s. Built as the *Leicestershire (above)*, a combination passenger-cargo ship with seventy-six berths used on the Liverpool-Rangoon run for Britain's Bibby Line, she became the Greek *Heraklion* in 1964 *(below)*. Her owners, the Typaldos Lines, were the fastest growing Greek passenger ship and ferry operators. Restyled for passenger-ferry service between Piraeus and Heraklion on Crete, she was in a stormy Aegean Sea when, on December 7, 1966, poorly-secured trucks and cars, and then a heavy truck, broke loose in the ship's holds. The bow loading door was rammed. It broke open and the ship flooded quickly. By the next morning, there was little trace of her other than floating debris. Out of 288 passengers and crew onboard, only forty-seven survived. They were found clutching floating pieces of wood and clinging to rocks on a nearby island. The Greek government quickly launched a major investigation and found that the *Heraklion* was unsafe (as were twelve of the other Typaldos passenger ships at the time), and that safety standards were lax and documents faked. The Typaldos fleet was seized, the owner sent to prison, and Greek maritime safety standards upgraded. [Built by Fairfield Shipbuilding & Engineering Company Limited, Glasgow, Scotland, 1949. 8,922 gross tons; 498 feet long; 60 feet wide. Steam turbines, single screw. Service speed 15.5 knots. 300 one-class passengers.]

PARAGUAY STAR. The *Paraguay Star* and her three sisters, the *Argentina Star*, *Brasil Star*, and *Uruguay Star* were the classic British combination passenger-cargo ships. Built to service the lucrative meat trade between London and Buenos Aires, they also carried passengers in intimate, almost club-like settings. The *Paraguay Star* is seen here *(above)* off-loading cargo at Rotterdam. But by the 1960s, the cargo was going to bigger, faster container ships, and travelers to the airlines. When the *Paraguay Star* caught fire while lying in the London docks in August 1969, there was little interest in restoring her. Instead, she was sold to Hamburg ship breakers. [Built by Cammell, Laird & Company, Birkenhead, England, 1948. 10,722 gross tons; 530 feet long; 68 feet wide. Steam turbines, single screw. Service speed 16 knots. 60 all-first-class passengers.]

GOTHIC. Another British combination passenger-cargo ship, the *Gothic* had an added distinction: she served as a royal yacht between 1953 and 1954 when she took Queen Elizabeth II on a celebratory, post-coronation world tour *(below)*. Normally used in the London–Panama–New Zealand service of the London-headquartered Shaw Savill Line, the *Gothic* was downgraded to cargo ship status by 1965. On August 2, 1968, during a voyage in the South Pacific, en route from Wellington to Liverpool, she caught fire. Seven of the crew perished. Temporary repairs kept her in service for another year before she was handed over to Taiwanese scrappers in August 1969. [Built by Swan, Hunter & Wigham Richardson Limited, Newcastle, England, 1948. 15,902 gross tons; 561 feet long; 72 feet wide. Steam turbines, twin screw. Service speed 17 knots. 85 all-first-class passengers.]

FAIRSEA. Created for low-fare tourist and immigrant services, the *Fairsea* was one of many post–World War II rebuilt passenger ships (*above*). She had been an American "baby flattop," a small, auxiliary aircraft carrier, but was soon loaned to Britain's Royal Navy and sailed as the HMS *Charger*. Unused in the late 1940s, she was bought by the Sitmar Line (a multinational shipping company) and rebuilt as the *Fairsea* for passenger sailings, mostly between Europe and Australia. An aging ship by 1969, however, she had an engine room fire during a long, ill-fated voyage between Papeete, Tahiti, and Balboa, Panama, on June 29. With 985 passengers and 250 crew onboard, she drifted in the Pacific for days, with dwindling water and supplies. A tug offered assistance but then broke down itself; then the captain became depressed and committed suicide. Finally, an American freighter, the *Louise Lykes*, towed the stricken *Fairsea* to Balboa. At a scant eight knots, the trip took eleven days. The weary passengers were flown onward from Panama to Europe, and the ship taken by a skeleton crew to La Spezia in Italy, where she was scrapped. [Built by Sun Shipbuilding & Dry Dock Company, Chester, Pennsylvania, 1941. 13,342 gross tons; 492 feet long; 69 feet wide. Doxford diesel, single screw. Service speed 16 knots. 1,460 all-tourist-class passengers.]

LA JANELLE. In a last-ditch effort to save and reuse an aging passenger ship, the *La Janelle* was to have a new life as a moored floating hotel/motel along the southern California coast. Fred Rodriguez visited the veteran liner off Port Hueneme, California, and recalled, "She had been anchored off the coast in April 1970 and was to be converted to a floating hotel/motel. But she was soon blown aground and then quickly sank on her seaward side. That August, using one of her lifeboats, I boarded the otherwise abandoned ship. I went aboard and later climbed her mast and walked along the stack. I also walked along the glass windows of the enclosed promenade deck. She was already being torn apart by the raging sea and a sandbar was building up against her as the ocean waters flowed in. I also entered the master's cabin and took a mirror and a small shelf, and climbed into the two-deck-high main lounge, which was being eaten apart by seawater."

Completed for New York–Caribbean service as the *Borinquen*, she was revived after the war as the *Puerto Rico* before becoming the transatlantic liner *Arosa Star* in 1954 (*below*). Sold again in 1959, she was renamed *Bahama Star* and became one of the earliest Miami-based cruise ships. She is seen in this view (*opposite, top*) while in dry dock at Jacksonville, Florida. Retired in 1968, she was sold yet again, renamed *La Janelle* and soon met her end off Port Hueneme. Her remains are seen in this view (*opposite, bottom*) from the summer of 1970. [Built by Bethlehem Steel Corporation, Quincy, Massachusetts, 1931. 7,114 gross tons; 466 feet long; 60 feet wide. Steam turbines, single screw. Service speed 15 knots. 735 all-first-class passengers.]

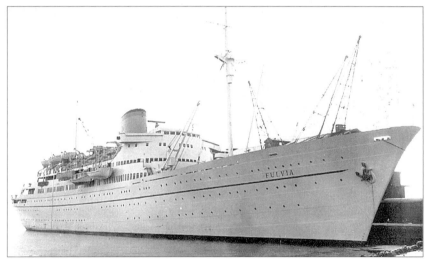

FULVIA. When completed in the fall of 1949, the *Oslofjord* was Norway's postwar flagship. She is seen here *(opposite, top)* in a view from May 1956, at Oslo, on her first meeting with her successor, the brand-new *Bergensfjord* (included in this work as the *Rasa Sayang*). Used in both North Atlantic as well as cruise service as the *Oslofjord* of the Norwegian America Line, her trade fell away such that she was time-chartered, beginning in 1969, for three years to Italy's Costa Line. She ran cruises, mostly from Genoa, as the renamed *Fulvia* *(opposite, middle)*. A ten-day summer cruise to the Atlantic Isles and Morocco proved to be her last. While sailing between Funchal and Tenerife on July 19, 1970, an engine room fire soon spread throughout the otherwise gleaming, all-white liner *(opposite, bottom)*. Abandoned, she sank thirty-six hours later. [Built by Netherlands Shipbuilding Company, Amsterdam, Holland, 1949. 16,844 gross tons; 577 feet long; 72 feet wide. Stork diesels, twin screw. Service speed 20 knots. 646 maximum cruise passengers.]

ANTILLES. "The *Antilles* was a tropical ship, a ship of the sun, a link to the colonies. She caught fire in the early evening, just before dinner. There was a great evacuation," recalled Steven Winograd, "but CGT [the French Line] acted too late. Spraying oil caused the fire. Simply, she had to be left, lying on the rocks at Mustique. She was a complete loss." James McNamara added, "I saw her at sea once and remember her as being a very beautiful, very handsome-looking ship." The *Antilles* is shown here *(above)* at Le Havre. During her regular Caribbean voyage, the *Antilles* caught fire on January 8, 1971. Abandoning ship, her 635 passengers and crew were rescued by the nearby *Queen Elizabeth 2* and two French Line freighters. Left on a reef, the blackened corpse of the ship broke in three and gradually fell into the sea. [Built by Naval Dockyard, Brest, France, 1952. 19,828 gross tons; 599 feet long; 80 feet wide. Steam turbines, twin screw. Service speed 22 knots. 778 passengers (404 first class, 285 cabin class, 89 tourist class).]

SEAWISE UNIVERSITY (ex-Queen Elizabeth). For thirty-two years, the *Queen Elizabeth* ranked as the largest liner afloat. With the *Queen Mary*, she was part of that legendary pair of ocean liners, the Cunard "Queens," as they were called *(above)*. They were heroic troopships during World War II and hugely successful Atlantic express super liners. They ran near-continuous five-day crossings between New York and Southampton with a stop at Cherbourg in each direction. But in the age of the jet, the *Queen Mary* was withdrawn in September 1967 and the *Queen Elizabeth* in October 1968. Even after her demise, the *Queen Elizabeth*'s size record remained, until eclipsed by the 101,000-ton cruise ship *Carnival Destiny* in 1996. She also endures as one of the best-looking liners ever to put to sea. "As the *Queen Elizabeth*, she might just have been the most balanced passenger ship ever built. She had great looks, the perfect profile," according to Steven Winograd. "She was uninspired on the inside, however. The *Queen Mary* was always the favorite."

While the *Queen Mary* found further life as a hotel and museum at Long Beach, near Los Angeles, the *Queen Elizabeth* was intended to have a similar role, but at Fort Lauderdale. The latter project failed entirely and in 1970 the giant ship was auctioned off (for $6 million) for conversion into a cruise ship/floating university. Renamed *Seawise University*, she was to make worldwide voyages, which included a return to New York in the fall of 1972. But on January 9, 1972, while anchored in Hong Kong harbor on the eve of her departure for final dry-docking in Japan, the former Cunard flagship caught fire. The blaze spread quickly. Some 900 workers and their families, onboard for a farewell party, escaped with only twenty-eight reported injuries. Later, reports suggested that the fire was a form of sabotage in the ongoing struggle between the Communist Chinese and the Taiwanese.

On January 10 the former *Queen Elizabeth* capsized, resting grotesquely at a sixty-five-degree angle (***above and below***). The Japanese were soon called and scrapped the wreckage in two years. Today, her underwater remains are covered by an ultramodern container terminal. "It was a tragic ending for a grand liner," said Charles Howland. "But I guess you could say that the end for most ships is seldom graceful. Mysterious fires and sinkings seem almost to be the norm." [Built by John Brown & Company Limited, 1936-40. 83,673 gross tons; 1,031 feet long; 118 feet wide. Steam turbines, quadruple screw. Service speed 28½ knots. 2,283 passengers in 1946 (823 first class, 662 cabin class, 798 tourist class).]

ORIENTAL WARRIOR. Fred Rodriguez remembered the *Oriental Warrior* and her five sisters from visits to New York. "She and her sisters were often docked at Pier 1 in Brooklyn Heights, just below the Brooklyn Bridge, and had their names illuminated in neon at night. They still carried passengers on their long trips to and from the Far East, and were among the great bargains of ocean travel at as little as $9 per person per day." Between 1953 and 1954, as part of their revival after the devastation of World War II, the Hamburg America Line and North German Lloyd each built three, high-standard combination passenger-cargo ships for their Europe–Far East operations. Although popular, the ships were outmoded by 1967 and sold to Hong Kong–based Orient Overseas Line. Hamburg America's former *Hamburg* became the *Oriental Warrior* and it was during a subsequent voyage, from New York to the Far East via Panama, that she met her end. On May 25, 1972, off Daytona Beach, Florida, a fire in the engine room spread quickly. Brought into Jacksonville (*above*), the ship soon sank, but was salvaged. Beyond economic repair, she was taken out to sea and deliberately scuttled on October 1. [Built by Bremer-Vulkan Shipyard, Bremen, West Germany, 1953. 9,000 gross tons; 538 feet long; 64 feet wide. MAN diesel, single screw. Service speed 16½ knots. 86 one-class passengers.]

METEOR. Although quite small, intimate, and certainly yacht-like, the Norwegian cruise ship *Meteor* had a select, loyal following *(above)*. She cruised the Norwegian fjords in summer, the Caribbean in winter, and the Mediterranean waters in spring and fall. By 1970 she began spending her summers in the lucrative Alaskan cruise trade, sailing from Vancouver. On one of these northern cruises, on May 22, 1971, she caught fire near Vancouver and was badly damaged. Although she was declared a total loss and expected to be scrapped, she was bought by Greece's Epirotiki Lines and restored for further cruising as the *Neptune (below)*. Laid up by 1998, she was not scrapped until 2003. [Built by Aalborg Vaerft Shipyard, Aalborg, Denmark, 1955. 2,856 gross tons; 297 feet long; 45 feet wide. Burmeister & Wain diesel, single screw. Service speed 17 knots. 147 all-first-class passengers.]

CARIBIA (ex-Caronia). In the summer of 2000, Andrew Kostantinides passed away. He was in his 80s and living at the time near Orlando in Florida. He was Greek and was involved in shipping. But many might ask, "Who was Andrew Kostantinides?" He certainly has a place in Greek passenger-ship history. Back in the late 1960s he bought from the Cunard Line what had once been one of the most celebrated and standard-setting luxury liners of her day, the *Caronia*. She had been the renowned "Green Goddess" and was noted for her long, luxurious cruises. She is shown here *(above)* arriving at New York's Pier 90 on her maiden voyage in January 1949. She had a club-like tone about her and some of her passengers, usually older ladies, lived onboard for months at a time. In fact, the all-time record holder for cruising, Miss Clara MacBeth, lived onboard the 34,100-ton ship for fourteen years! Kostantinides bought the ship when Cunard, faced with jet competition, mounting operational costs, and therefore huge losses, was quickly downsizing between 1967 and 1968. The 715-foot-long *Caronia*, always expensive to operate and always more the prestige piece than moneymaker, was on the disposal list.

"Everyone seems to have fond memories of the *Caronia*. She seemed to always be a happy ship," according to Steven Winograd. "When first built, she sent a message that the British are back. Luxury had returned even if there were still rations back home. Yet the *Caronia* was rich and plentiful, full of excitement and the glamour of the country club before dinner. You could almost hear the cocktail shakers from shoreside. Capped by that very pleasing, massive funnel, and painted in her distinctive greens, she was the most expensive ship of her day. She was always in the right place at the right time, warm waters in winter and in Scandinavia during summer. Of course, she herself was the ultimate right place to be!"

Kostantinides formed the Universal Line, a Greek firm using a Panama flag and one with high hopes of running seven- and fourteen-day cruises out of New York with the ex-*Caronia* (renamed *Caribia*). Kostantinides was the owner, as well as the most visible member, of the new company. "There were secret partners in Universal and these included Cunard itself as well as the Chandris Lines," according to marine surveyor Arthur Crook, who was contracted to assist in the conversion of the 1948-built liner. "But Kostantinides was the front man, the so-called owner. His whole family was actually connected with the *Caribia*. There was also Portuguese money involved."

After being laid up at Southampton for a time with a rumored sale to Yugoslavian interests known as Dumas Turist (who were said to want the ship for use as a floating hotel along the Dalmatian coast), the 930-passenger *Caronia* was finally sold to Kostantinides' Universal Line. She set off for Piraeus and some refitting and repairs at Perama. The once familiar exterior shades of green disappeared when the hull and the upper decks were painted over in white. The large single stack, once the largest afloat, was also redone in white, but with a blue band at the top.

"The *Caronia/Caribia* had the underwater body of a battleship. She was very strong and very heavy," added Crook. "But she also had turbine problems. Once, in her Cunard days, she had to sail empty because of so much vibration caused by the machinery. Mr Kostantinides took a great personal interest in the ship and her rejuvenation, and used to come over to Perama every day from Piraeus. He arrived on water skis and boarded the ship by ladder."

In the fall of 1968, the twenty-two-knot *Caribia* set off for Naples, but she soon ran into trouble. "There were at least two fires between Piraeus and Naples. One blaze was in the funnel," said Crook, who was aboard at the time. "The initial crew was a mix of Greeks, Turks, Italians, and three Brits, and all of them hated each other. The Turks brought on live sheep at Piraeus and used them for slaughter. Later, the scuppers were filled with discarded bones. We arrived in Naples with a list and stayed there for weeks for further repairs. The boilers needed to be re-tubed among other pressing problems. I remember lots of crew parties using the last of the Cunard wines."

In January 1969 the *Caribia* started cruising out of New York to the sunny Caribbean, but her posted schedules were short-lived, in fact very short-lived. On the second trip, while off Martinique, there was a serious engine room explosion and subsequent breakdown. The passengers had to be flown home and the ship towed back to New York. She languished about the harbor. She was at the Todd shipyard in Brooklyn's Erie Basin, then at nearby Bush Terminal, at anchor in the Lower Bay, laid up between Piers 84 and 86, and finally moored at Pier 56, coincidentally a former Cunard terminal (until 1950), located at the foot of West 14th Street. The *Caribia* was reported to be for sale. Among others, both the Chandris and Lauro lines were said to want her for further service. Kostantinides himself hinted of further service, but on reduced, cheaply priced three- and four-day cruises. But as more and more time passed, the once impeccable ship slipped into irretrievable

decay. On a bitterly cold day in February 1974 with little hope in sight and with creditors of all sorts pressing for payment, she was opened to the general public for a special sale: an auction of her fittings, from furniture to china, from wood panels to kitchen pots. Everything was tagged except the remains of the dead rats that could be seen in otherwise darkened pantries and back stairwells. Hundreds bought items, often at very reasonable prices, and one couple bought enough to start a trendy, Deco-style restaurant on lower Fifth Avenue in Greenwich Village. "Kostantinides had run out of money and, between 1973 and 1974, he even sold off the remaining fuel in the ship's tanks," added Arthur Crook. "He even tried to sell the water ballast at $100 a ton!" James McNamara added, "As the *Caronia*, she was one of the finest, most luxurious liners of her time. She set standards for seagoing luxury with food, service, and style. So it was especially sad to see her in her final years. She was like a 'bag lady,' loitering about without a home and steadily declining at the same time."

On April 27, 1974, under the guidance of a sturdy oceangoing tug, the rust-stained *Caribia* set off for the Far East, to Taiwan, and the scrappers (*above*). But her woes continued. During a fierce storm, she was thrown onto a breakwater at Guam [on August 13] and broke in three pieces. Her remains, declared a menace by the U.S. Coast Guard, were soon cut up and hauled away (*below*).

I spoke with Andrew Kostantinides by phone in the summer of 1999. He was quite pleasant and agreed to an interview. Alas, other projects got in the way. Time passed too quickly. A further chat never took place. I wonder what other facts, notations, and insights he might have provided and perhaps "rewritten" on the story of the former *Caronia*. [Built by John Brown & Company Limited, Clydebank, Scotland, 1948. 34,183 gross tons; 715 feet long; 91 feet wide. Steam turbines, twin screw. Service speed 22 knots. 932 passengers as built (581 first class, 351 tourist class).]

CARIBIA (ex-Vulcania). As the *Vulcania*, she was one of the most popular and long lasting of all Italian liners. She sailed for thirty-five years, beginning with the Cosulich Line and then the Italian Line on the Atlantic run between Trieste, Venice, other Mediterranean ports, and New York. At the end of World War II she was in American hands, serving as an Allied troopship. The *Vulcania* was returned to the Italians in 1946 and sailed for the Italian Line until 1965. She then changed hands, transferring to other Italians, the Grimaldi-Siosa Lines, who sailed her as the *Caribia* in Europe-Caribbean and Mediterranean cruise services. She is seen here *(above)* at Valletta on Malta. Wearing out, however, her engines failed during a cruise of the western Mediterranean in September 1972. The ship lost control and hit a reef at Cannes and, coincidentally, at almost exactly the same spot where another Siosa liner, the *Venezuela*, had gone aground in 1962. Patched up, the veteran *Caribia* was far too old for expensive repairs and was towed to Genoa, sold to Spanish ship breakers, and then resold to Taiwanese scrap dealers. Towed out to Kaohsiung, she was awaiting a berth, in the summer of 1974, when she sprang leaks and flooded. Pumped out, she was eventually brought into port and broken up. [Built by Cantieri Navale Triestino, Monfalcone, Italy, 1928. 24,496 gross tons; 631 feet long; 80 feet wide. Fiat diesels, twin screw. Service speed 21 knots. 1,437 passengers (337 first class, 368 cabin class, 732 tourist class).]

HOMERIC. "The fire damages aboard the immensely popular, still useful *Homeric* could have been repaired, but once again it was the smell of smoke, the lingering stench of it, that remained behind the paneling. This could not have been removed, at least not without expensive repairs and restoration, and since the ship was thirty-three years old at the time, it finished her," noted Captain James McNamara.

Built in 1931 as the first of three sisters for San Francisco–based Matson Line, she was then completed as the *Mariposa* and sailed the long-haul service from California to the South Seas and Australia. Used as a trooper during the war, she was laid up afterward until 1953. She was then sold to Home Lines, raising the Panamanian colors as their flagship *Homeric*. She ran North Atlantic service for about nine months of the year and then went cruising from New York to the Caribbean for the remainder. Her capacity had almost doubled from her Matson days. "She was American-built and was so solid," noted Steven Winograd. "She was designed and constructed to go on forever. Typically, such ships had three or four lives. And as the *Homeric*, she had great style. You could almost smell the Italian breadsticks when still on the pier. Your mouth watered. She was a gastronomic explosion yet also comfortable and homey. There were no pretensions about the *Homeric*. She had huge loyalty from passengers as well as crew. And I remember her looking so elegant at night when sailing from a Caribbean port. Her twin funnels were aglow." While outbound on a summer Caribbean cruise from New York in July 1973, the *Homeric* suffered a fire off the New Jersey coast. She returned to port, her subsequent sailings were canceled, and the ship was sent empty to Genoa and laid up. She is seen here (**opposite, bottom**) to the left of another scrap-bound passenger ship, the *Caribia 2*. The 43-year-old ship was sold to Taiwanese ship breakers in 1974. [Built by Bethlehem Steel Company, Quincy, Massachusetts, 1931. 24,907 gross tons; 638 feet long; 79 feet wide. Steam turbines, twin screw. Service speed 20 knots. 1,243 maximum passengers; 730 all-first-class for cruises.]

MALAYSIA KITA. Among the most handsome combination passenger-cargo liners of their day, the *Viet-Nam* and her two twin sisters, the *Cambodge* and *Laos*, were built for the Marseilles–Far East service of Messageries Maritimes. In 1968, the *Viet-Nam* (**above**) was renamed *Pacifique*. She and the *Laos* were sold to Panamanian-flag interests, but with interests in eastern Moslem pilgrim services, and the *Pacifique* became the *Malaysia Baru* and then the *Malaysia Kita* for service mostly between Singapore and Jeddah. She caught fire on May 12, 1974, while undergoing repairs in Singapore. She later sank, after being towed to the outer harbor. A difficult salvage followed and she was not raised until the summer of 1975. She was sold a year later for breaking up at Kaohsiung on Taiwan. Coincidentally, the former *Laos*, which became the *Empress Abeto* and then *Malaysia Raya*, burned out at Port Klang in Malaysia on August 24, 1976. Her remains were later scrapped on Taiwan as well. [Built by Chantiers de la Ciotat, La Ciotat, France, 1952. 11,792 gross tons; 532 feet long; 72 feet wide. Steam turbines, twin screw. Service speed 21 knots. Approximately 1,612 one-class passengers.]

CUNARD AMBASSADOR. By the late 1960s, the historic Cunard Line wanted to enter the lucrative, mass-market cruise business and so built two small cruise ships, the *Cunard Adventurer* and *Cunard Ambassador*. Although small, they seemed distant cousins to the *Queen Mary* and *Queen Elizabeth*, and even the brand-new *Queen Elizabeth 2*. The *Cunard Ambassador* had a short Cunard career, however. On September 12, 1974, on a positioning voyage from Miami to New Orleans, she caught fire. No passengers were aboard. Brought into Key West, she was declared a loss, but sold to Danish buyers, who rebuilt her as the sheep carrier *Linda Clausen (above)*. In 1980, she became the *Procyon* and then, in 1983, the *Raslan*. Fire claimed her completely on July 11, 1983, and two years later the remains were scrapped on Taiwan. [Built by Rotterdam Dry Dock Company, Rotterdam, Holland, 1972. 14,155 gross tons; 484 feet long; 71 feet wide. Diesels, twin screw. Service speed 20.5 knots. 806 all-first-class passengers.]

RASA SAYANG. Built as the *Bergensfjord* for Norwegian America Line's transatlantic and cruise service, this fine-looking liner was sold to the French Line in 1971, a replacement for the aforementioned *Antilles*, and renamed *De Grasse*. Used mostly for cruising, she was sold again in 1973, becoming the Norwegian-owned *Rasa Sayang*, but for cruising out of Singapore *(opposite, top)*. Damaged by a serious fire in 1977, she was repaired, but then soon sold again, becoming the Greek-owned *Golden Moon*. A plan to sail her as the Dutch-chartered *Prins van Oranje* followed, but soon failed and instead she was set to resume Far Eastern cruising as the revived *Rasa Sayang*. But on August 27, 1980, while being refitted at Perama in Greece, she caught fire and was destroyed. Her smoldering remains were later towed to the shallow waters of the harbor and then allowed to capsize *(opposite, bottom)*. The wreckage remains there to this day. [Built by Swan, Hunter & Wigham Richardson Limited, Wallsend-on-Tyne, England, 1956. 18,739 gross tons; 578 feet long; 72 feet wide. Stork diesels, twin screw. Service speed 20 knots. 878 maximum passengers as built; 420 all-first-class for cruises.]

ANGELINA LAURO (ex-Oranje). "The design of the *Oranje* was revolutionary. The vessel had a pot-belly-shaped hull, resulting in architectural compromise between a tonnage as low as possible and sufficient space for three large diesels and fuel storage," noted Dr. Nico Guns. "The powerful diesels, each one driving a screw, would make her the fastest motor ship in the world." Captain James McNamara noted, "I visited her in the 1950s as the *Oranje* and she was a beautiful ship. She represented the great age of the colonial ocean liner and was built to serve between Holland and the Dutch East Indies." Used on the Amsterdam–East Indies run of the Nederland Line, she was sold to Italy's Lauro Line in 1964 and rebuilt completely as the modern *Angelina Lauro (above)*. Another Dutch liner, the *Willem Ruys*, changed hands as well and became the same company's *Achille Lauro*. During their conversions in Italy, both ships survived serious fires. Onboard the *Angelina Lauro* in a Genoa dockyard, six workmen lost their lives. By the 1970s she was cruising most of the time, the Mediterranean in summer, the Caribbean for the remainder. At St. Thomas, on March 30, 1979, while her passengers were ashore, a galley fire gutted the ship *(opposite, top)*. She listed to port *(opposite, bottom)*. Refloated that summer, she too was an aged ship beyond expensive and extensive repairs. She was sold to the Taiwanese for scrapping. But while empty and under tow in the Pacific on September 24, she sank. [Built by Netherlands Shipbuilding Company, Amsterdam, Holland, 1939. 24,377 gross tons; 672 feet long; 83 feet wide. Sulzer diesels, triple screw. Service speed 21½ knots. 1,616 maximum passengers; approximately 900 one-class on cruises.]

BONAIRE STAR. Built as part of West German reparations to Israel, the *Jerusalem* and her twin sister, the *Theodor Herzl* (listed in this book as the *Fiesta*), were created for the busy inter-Mediterranean service. They traded between Marseilles, other ports, and Haifa. The *Jerusalem* was also used as a winter cruise ship, sailing from New York to the Caribbean. She is seen here (*above*) outbound along the East River. Zim Lines used a terminal in Greenpoint, Brooklyn, until 1961. In 1966 she became the *Miami*, sailing for Florida-based P&O Steamship Lines on three-and four-day cruises to the Bahamas. Two years later, she was renamed *New Bahama Star* for another Miami firm, Eastern Steamship Lines. Her name was later shortened to *Bahama Star*, but by 1975 she was sold yet again, supposedly to become a Venezuelan-based cruise ship, the *Bonaire Star*. Nothing came to pass and instead she was sold to Taiwanese ship breakers. On the tow out to Kaohsiung the empty ship sank in the Pacific on October 3, 1979. [Built by Deutsche Werft, Hamburg, West Germany, 1957. 9,914 gross tons; 488 feet long; 65 feet wide. Steam turbines, twin screw. Service speed 19 knots. 570 all-tourist-class passengers as built.]

LEONARDO DA VINCI. "The *Leonardo da Vinci* was a fantastic ship! She was the Queen Bee of Italian shipping," noted Steven Winograd. "She was every bit the embodiment of her nation, her name alone carried huge status. She had a big-ship personality. And although she was a huge fuel burner and a money loser, no expense was spared in her luxuries. She was allowed to run down in later years, however, and was a ship of rust, worn carpets, and a somber tone." Fred Rodriguez remembered her as well. "She was a beautiful ship with very gracious lines. I remember that up near the pilothouse there was a big, brass Catholic mural. It was a sort of shrine that looked like the traditional builder's plate. All the Italian Line passenger ships seemed to have these and they were supposed to be a good luck touch."

The splendid *Leonardo da Vinci*, seen here (*opposite, top*) passing the *Vulcania* in the mid-Atlantic, ran the last of the celebrated Italian Line's transatlantic crossings when she sailed from New York to Genoa in June 1976. After a short stint doing Florida cruises, she was laid up at La Spezia in September 1978, sadly never to sail again. Rumors that she would be sold and possibly sail once more came to nothing. On July 3, 1980, a fire broke out in the ship's chapel and spread quickly. She was towed outside the main harbor, burned herself out, then heeled over with a sixty-degree list. She was raised in March 1981 and scrapped locally in 1982 (*opposite, middle and bottom*). "I was vacationing in Italy when the *Leonardo da Vinci* caught fire," remembered Charles Howland. "Of course, it was front-page news, but I can't say it was greeted by surprise. Mysterious fires seemed almost to be the norm. The *Leonardo da Vinci* was unquestionably a beautiful ship, but never replaced the *Andrea Doria* in my affection." [Built by Ansaldo Shipyards, Genoa, Italy, 1960. 33,340 gross tons; 761 feet long; 92 feet wide. Steam turbines, twin screw. Service speed 23 knots. 1,326 passengers (413 first class, 342 cabin class, 571 tourist class).]

PRINSENDAM. "The loss of the *Prinsendam* was very embarrassing to the Holland America Line, which had a superb reputation," reported the late Everett Viez. "But the ship itself was really a misfit in the fleet, much like the *Cunard Adventurer* and *Cunard Ambassador* were to Cunard at about the same time. They did not match their predecessors in size, style, or standard. And the *Prinsendam* was the first Holland-America liner to have an Indonesian hotel staff." Used in Alaskan cruise service from Vancouver during the summers and in Indonesian service from Singapore for the remainder, she was on a positioning trip, from Vancouver to the Far East, when she caught fire in the Gulf of Alaska in October 1980 (*above and below*). The ship was abandoned, and the exceptional efforts of the American and Canadian Coast Guard forces saved all passengers and crew. Days later, after salvage attempts failed, she was allowed to sink. [Built by De Merwede Shipyard, Hardinxveld, Holland, 1973. 8,566 gross tons; 427 feet long; 62 feet wide. Werkspor diesels, twin screw. Service speed 21 knots. 374 maximum cruise passengers.]

REINA DEL MAR. In 1951 she was called the "largest liner designed primarily for cruising," in light of the fact that Cunard's famed *Caronia* was at first considered a ship that made cruises as well as Atlantic crossings. The 13,600-ton *Ocean Monarch* of the Furness-Bermuda Line, an arm of Britain's Furness, Withy & Company, was an instant success. She was the ideal ship: well designed, popular, and very profitable. She ended her days in Greek hands, however, renamed the *Reina del Mar*, reviving the name of another very popular British liner, the 1956-built *Reina del Mar* of Pacific Steam Navigation and later Union-Castle.

The 516-foot-long *Ocean Monarch* was built as a deliberate replacement for the celebrated *Monarch of Bermuda*, a three-stacker well known in the 1930s, which had burned out during her postwar refit in 1947. She was thought to be a complete loss and so Furness abandoned their rights. She was repaired and became the migrant ship *New Australia* and later the Greek Line's *Arkadia*. Her original near-sister, the *Queen of Bermuda*, still needed a companion for the busy New York–Bermuda trade, and so the 440-passenger *Ocean Monarch* was created. But Furness was also interested in further cruise voyages, two-week trips deeper into the Caribbean and in summer to the Canadian Maritimes and the St. Lawrence River. She sailed into New York to a grand reception in April 1951.

She had the perfect cruise ship amenities: complete air-conditioning, a pool deck, smart public rooms, and every cabin with a private bath. She was, however, soon facing stiffer competition from bigger and newer liners (such as Home Lines' spectacular *Oceanic* by 1965) but also more stringent U.S. Coast Guard safety

standards. In 1966, Furness decided that the thirty-three-year-old *Queen of Bermuda* and the *Ocean Monarch*, by then reaching middle age, were not worth costly refits. The *Queen of Bermuda* understandably went to the breakers while the *Ocean Monarch* was, after a short lay up, sold to new owners, Bulgaria's Balkanturist Company. Renamed *Varna*, she was used primarily for overseas charter cruising. In the early 1970s she spent her summers on lease to the Gala Navigation Company, running cruises out of Montreal to ports along the St. Lawrence, to the Maritime Provinces, and occasionally down to familiar waters: Bermuda. But the greatly increased fuel oil prices between 1973 and 1974 sent her into layup.

In 1978 she was sold to Greek buyers and moved to Perama Bay to await reactivation. A year later, she was to be renamed *Riviera* for eastern Mediterranean cruises out of Venice, but these never materialized. Then there was a plan by the so-called World Cruise Line to run her as the *Venus* on New York–Bermuda cruises. This too never developed. Between 1980 and 1981, her owners, now identified as Dolphin-Hellas Shipping Company, released a brochure detailing European cruises, to the Mediterranean, the Norwegian fjords, and western Europe, for the *Reina del Mar*. The ex-*Varna*, ex–*Ocean Monarch* began her refit at Perama (*above*), but on May 28, 1981, she was destroyed by fire and then capsized. She was a total loss, a pathetic end for such a fine little liner. [Built by Vickers-Armstrong Limited, Newcastle, England, 1951. 13,581 gross tons; 516 feet long; 73 feet wide. Steam turbines, twin screw. Service speed 18 knots. 600 cruise passengers.]

ATLANTIS. Yacht-like in appearance, this Greek cruise ship, owned by the K Lines (Kavounides Shipping Company), had been built first as a ferry, the *Adonis*, but was later rebuilt as the *Atlantis* for mostly eastern Mediterranean cruising. She was lost to fire, however, while undergoing repairs at Perama in Greece in March 1983 (*above*). Her remains were soon scrapped. [Built by Cantieri Riuniti dell'Adriatico, Monfalcone, Italy, 1965. 5,000 gross tons; 318 feet long; 52 feet wide. Sulzer diesels, twin screw. Service speed 17 knots. 322 cruise passengers.]

COLUMBUS C. "The *Kungsholm* of 1953 was one of the most beautifully proportioned and handsomely decorated liners of all time," said Captain James McNamara. "She was just about ocean liner perfection!" Steven Winograd agreed. "She was one of the best looking liners ever and even better as the *Europa*. She looked great with her black hull and twin mustard funnels. She was a smaller ship, but with a big-ship feel. Once aboard, you felt you were actually in Germany. The music from her decks and lounges filled the night air when she made her midnight sailings from Manhattan's West Side. She would be strung with lights and was always immaculate. North German Lloyd in the 1960s had some of the best fed and best served liners afloat." As Swedish America Line's *Kungsholm*, she was sold to North German Lloyd in 1965 and became their *Europa*. Costa Cruises bought her in 1981 and sailed her as the *Columbus C* (**opposite, bottom**). On July 29, 1984, during a Mediterranean cruise, she was blown by high winds against a breakwater at Cadiz in Spain. Attempting to dock and off-load her passengers, she later flooded at the pier, canting to starboard for a time. After being righted, she settled in an upright posi-

tion (**above**). Unfortunately, she was beyond repair and was scrapped in Spain in 1985. [Built by De Schelde Shipyard, Flushing, Holland, 1953. 21,141 gross tons; 600 feet long; 77 feet wide. Burmeister & Wain diesels, twin screw. Service speed 19 knots. 802 passengers as built (176 first class, 626 tourist class).]

MIKHAIL LERMONTOV. Fred Rodriguez visited the *Mikhail Lermontov* (**below**) and other Soviet liners during their visits to New York in the 1970s. "It was always a little tense onboard ships such as the *Mikhail Lermontov*. It was still the Soviet era and KGB agents were said to be aboard," he remembered. "There was also a distance between the crew and passengers and guests. They could not seem to be too friendly. There was a sort of uneasiness. She was not a remarkable ship in any way, but had a simple, but comfortable interior." Used for cruising in later years, she ran aground and sank in New Zealand waters on February 16, 1986. [Built by Mathias-Thesen Werft, Wismar, East Germany, 1971. 19,872 gross tons; 578 feet long; 77 feet wide. Sulzer diesels, twin screw. Service speed 20 knots. 700 all-one-class passengers).]

UGANDA. The *Uganda (above)* was created for the declining British–East African colonial trade, sailing between London, Mombasa, and other ports. She was rebuilt between 1967 and 1968 as an educational cruise ship. Operated by London-based British India Cruises, she served as a hospital ship during the Falklands War in 1982. She resumed cruising afterward, but was laid up in 1985. Sold to Taiwanese scrappers, she capsized outside Kaohsiung harbor during a typhoon in August 1986. [Built by Barclay Curle & Company Limited, Glasgow, Scotland, 1952. 16,907 gross tons; 540 feet long; 7l feet wide. Steam turbines, twin screw. Service speed 16 knots. 1,226 passengers as a cruise ship (306 adults, 920 students).]

ADMIRAL NAKHIMOV. The *Berlin* of 1925 was one of the smaller, more intermediate German passenger ships built after World War I. She represented the more moderate pace of her owners, North German Lloyd, as they reemerged as an Atlantic passenger operator. Copied to some extent from the earlier, but larger *Columbus*, the combined investment would lead, within four years, to the giant, high-speed sisters *Bremen* and *Europa*. Sadly, the *Berlin* would have a very tragic end; not for the Germans, but for the Soviets.

In October 1937 she made interesting and mysterious headlines at New York. The 15,200-ton passenger ship was loaded with 6,000 tons of scrap metal, obviously sold to the Nazi government, but through intermediaries. She then sailed from Pier 84 without even a single passenger. Just two weeks before, another Nazi-German liner, Hamburg America's *St. Louis*, had loaded 3,000 tons of scrap and then she too sailed eastbound without passengers. During the war, the 572-foot-long *Berlin* was a Nazi-operated hospital ship, but then struck a mine and sank off Swinemunde on February 1, 1945. She was underwater for nearly four years before the Soviets, claiming the wreckage, successfully salvaged the ship and began an eight-year restoration and refit. She reemerged in 1957 as the all-

white, squat-stacked *Admiral Nakhimov* (**opposite, bottom**), trading mostly in the local Black Sea trades out of Odessa, and with an occasional crossing to Havana in later years. It was during a mini cruise on September 15, 1986, that the sixty-one-year-old ship met her end. Forty-five minutes after leaving the port of Novorossisk, she was rammed by another Soviet ship, the 41,000-ton bulk carrier *Pyotr Velev*. The former *Berlin* sank within eight minutes and nearly 400 passengers and crew drowned in what was called one of the worst peacetime shipping disasters in Soviet history. The masters of both ships were later found to be at fault and were given prison sentences. [Built by Bremer Vulkan Shipyard, Vegesack, Germany, 1925. 17,053 gross tons; 572 feet long; 69 feet wide. Steam triple-expansion engines, twin screw. Service speed 16 knots. 870 one-class passengers.]

JUPITER. The *Jupiter* (**above**) was a Mediterranean cruise ship and one of the most popular ships in the Epirotiki fleet. While she is perhaps best remembered for her Aegean Sea cruises out of Piraeus, which included calls in Egypt, Israel, and Turkey, she also traveled on special charters to the western Mediterranean, Scandinavia, and the Caribbean. In the fall of 1998 her career came to an abrupt, premature end. On October 21 while carrying 500 students and their teachers as passengers on an educational cruise charter, she was rammed by an Italian car carrier just outside Piraeus harbor. She sank within forty minutes with a loss of four people.

The 7,811-ton, 415-foot-long *Jupiter*, once the flagship and largest ship of the Epirotiki fleet, had been built at Nantes in France in 1961. She was then part of an enthusiastic building program for the Israelis, for the state-owned Zim Israel Navigation Company, the Zim Lines. Named *Moledet*, she was built with 596 all-tourist-class berths for the busy, mostly migrant, and low-fare tourist trade between Marseilles and Haifa. There were also calls in Italy and sometimes in Greece, and occasional sailings out of the Adriatic from Venice. But when inter-Mediterranean passenger services were overtaken by aircraft, and as migration by sea to Israel sagged, the *Moledet* was out of work. She had less than ten years of service with Zim. She was sold to Epirotiki in 1970 and rebuilt for cruising. Efthymiadis Lines had been bidding for her and the Stena Line was said to be interested as well. She was fitted with very comfortable quarters for up to 450 passengers. All of the cabins now had at least a private shower and toilet, and the public areas were enhanced by contemporary art with a Greek history and mythology theme. She was to have been renamed *Zeus*, but the name *Jupiter* was selected in time for her maiden cruise from Piraeus in April 1971. Oddly, however, the name *Zeus* remained, painted only on her stern.

Between 1985 and 1986, there was a general decline in Mediterranean cruising caused by terrorism in the Middle East, political troubles caused by the Libyans and the headline-making hijacking of the Italian liner *Achille Lauro*. The *Jupiter*, like many other Greek cruise ships at the time, spent much time in layup at anchor in Perama Bay, because there were simply too few passengers. In 1987, it was reported that she had actually been sold to new owners and was to be renamed *Caribbean Prince*, but this never materialized. Instead, she remained with Epirotiki—mostly for educational cruising, carrying British students and their teachers. Sadly, her loss was the first of four in succession for her owners. [Built by Chantiers de l'Atlantique, St. Nazaire, France, 1961. 7,811 gross tons; 415 feet long; 65 feet wide. SEMT Pielstick diesel, single screw. Service speed 16 knots. 473 cruise passengers.]

LAVIA. Built as the combination passenger-cargo liner *Media* for Cunard Line's New York–Liverpool service, she was sold to Italy's Cogedar Line in 1961 and rebuilt as *Flavia* for Europe-Australia service. Later used by Costa as a cruise ship, she was sold to Chinese buyers in 1982 and renamed *Flavian* and then *Lavia*. She burned at Hong Kong on January 7, 1989 *(above)*, and was scrapped on Taiwan later that same year. [Built by John Brown & Company Limited, Clydebank, Scotland, 1947. 15,465 gross tons; 556 feet long; 70 feet wide. Steam turbines, twin screw. Service speed 18 knots. 1,120 maximum passengers.]

OCEANOS. The *Jean Laborde*, one of four combination passenger-cargo ships for Messageries Maritimes' Marseilles–East Africa–Indian Ocean service was sold to the Greek-flag Efthymiadis Lines in 1970. This ship took on a succession of names: *Mykinai*, *Ancona*, *Brindisi Express*, and *Eastern Princess* before becoming the *Oceanos* in 1976 for other Greeks, the Epirotiki Lines *(below)*. A refitted, upgraded cruise ship, she was used in diverse, often charter services. Unfortunately, she had a tragic, very dramatic end. During a South African cruise, on a voyage between east London and Durban, she began to leak, then flooded, and finally lost power. She sank in very rough seas on August 4, 1991. All passengers and crew were rescued. [Built by Forges et Chantiers de la Gironde, Bordeaux, France, 1951. 7,554 gross tons; 492 feet long; 64 feet wide. Burmeister & Wain diesels, twin screw. Service speed 17 knots. 500 cruise passengers.]

PEGASUS. In 1984, Seattle-based Stanley McDonald decided to return to the cruise business. He was, of course, something of a cruise industry legend. He had been the creator of the original Princess Cruises back in the mid-1960s, which he later sold to Britain's P&O Group. His latest venture was called Sundance Cruises, for which he purchased the 12,500-ton ferry *Svea Corona*. Restyled as the cruise ship *Sundancer*, she had barely begun her first Alaskan cruise season from Vancouver when in June 1984 she went aground, nearly sank, and was finally declared a total loss. But Greek buyers, the Epirotiki Lines, had other ideas. They bought her, towed her to Greece, and then refitted her as the *Pegasus*. She is seen here (*above*) leaving Vancouver under tow for Greece, on December 1, 1984. In June 1991 there were yet more troubles for the 499-foot-long ship. She burned out at Venice, was declared a complete loss, laid up, and finally scrapped at Aliaga in Turkey in March 1995.

When first built by the French in 1975, she carried 1,200 passengers (800 in cabins, another 400 in reclining, aircraft-style chairs) as well as 290 cars. She then sailed for the Swedish-flag Silja Line and ranked as one of the largest ferries afloat. She traded on the overnight Baltic Sea run, shuttling between Stockholm and Helsinki. The *Svea Corona* was later surpassed by newer, far larger tonnage and was sold to Sundance and refitted for North American West Coast cruising: summers in Alaska, winters along the Mexican Riviera. But she barely began her first published schedule. "The *Sundancer* seemed to have trouble from the beginning," recalled Giuseppe Lovece, then a waiter aboard. "On the delivery voyage from Miami to Vancouver, we had refrigerator problems in Panama. All the crew had to carry food ashore. But it was during our third Alaska cruise that the ship was finished for Sundance."

"We were sailing along the Inside Passage [in June 1984] and had just had our 'Welcome Aboard Night' celebrations," added Lovece. "It was midnight. I felt a bang and the ship suddenly began to list. The alarms sounded. I went out on deck and, surprisingly, saw a tree pressed against the railing. We were aground. I returned to my cabin just as water was rushing in the lower stairwells. Inside my cabin, the water was quickly up to my knees. The ship was listing slowly at first and then quite quickly. The restaurant tables, the dishes, and the cutlery seemed to be flying around! But very carefully, the captain was trying to reach the opposite shore where there was a pier. But it was pitch dark, the middle of the night, and the *Sundancer* then rammed a barge loaded with logs. More trouble!"

Declared a constructive total loss and about to be sold to scrap merchants, the twenty-one-knot ship suggested at least some potential to Epirotiki engineers. Towed to Piraeus via Panama, she was restored as the cruise ship *Pegasus*. Afterward, she did considerable cruising: the Greek isles, the Caribbean, and the east coast of South America. There were reports that she would be used for one-night "party cruises" out of New York in the summer of 1991, but these never materialized. At the time of the fire (1991), she was actually under charter and serving as an industrial display ship for a German electronics firm. Her intended summertime Aegean cruises were transferred to another ship, Med Sun Lines' *Atalante*, which Epirotiki temporarily renamed *Homericus*. After a long debate about her future, the *Pegasus* was finally sold for scrap. [Built by Dubigeon-Normandie SA, Nantes, France, 1975. 12,600 gross tons; 499 feet long; 73 feet wide. Pielstick diesels, twin screw. Service speed 22 knots. 810 cruise passengers.]

FIESTA. Despite the infirmities of old age, such as decreasing economic efficiency often complicated by mechanical woes, ship owners sometimes see hope, and sometimes lots of it, in secondhand passenger ships. Greek ship owners, in particular, have had a long track record in this area. Often, they work complete wonders with older, tired ships. One example was the case of the newly formed Fiesta Cruise Lines, an arm of Greece's Ambassador Cruises. They had high hopes for the 9,900-ton, thirty-five-year-old *Fiesta*, the former Israeli ship, *Theodor Herzl* (*opposite, top*). She had been brought over to Greece after being laid up in Florida and, once moored in Perama Bay near Piraeus, her resurrection and facelift began. She was to emerge as yet another "new" cruise ship, taking travelers around the eastern Mediterranean in summers and through Caribbean waters in wintertime. But it all went astray on October 24, 1991, when the 487-foot-long ship caught fire, burned out and capsized, overloaded with firefighters' water. Repairs were ruled out almost from the start, so the salvage was scrapped (*opposite, bottom*).

"The *Vera Cruz* (her name when *Fiesta* was owned by Bermuda Star Lines) was not a great favorite of mine. She was too small and not really a good representative of a nation," added Steven Winograd. "In her days as the *Theodor Herzl*, she seemed a distant ship, one not seen in New York except maybe once or twice." Fred Rodriguez added, "The *Vera Cruz* was a nice, little, almost toylike cruise ship. I sailed her several times and recall once, as we passed through the Cape Cod Canal in high winds, she emerged unharmed. She was really a very good 'sea boat.' During a slack spell in 1981, I recall her being laid up for several weeks over in Port Newark, New Jersey." [Built by Deutsche Werft, Hamburg, West Germany, 1957. 10,595 gross tons; 487 feet long; 64 feet wide. Steam turbines, twin screw. Service speed 18 knots. 960 maximum cruise passengers.]

DANAE. Built as the freighter *Port Melbourne* for Britain's Port Line, she was sold to the Greek-flag Carras Group, who intended to rebuild her as the ferry *Therisos Express*. The plans were shelved and instead she was rebuilt in 1974 as the cruise ship *Danae* (*above*). Sold to Costa Cruises in 1985, the ship was badly damaged by a fire at Genoa in December 1991 and declared a loss. She was resold, however, becoming the Greek-owned *Baltica*, then the *Switzerland* for Swiss Cruise Lines and sails today as the *Princess Danae* for Lisbon-based Classic Cruises International. [Built by Harland & Wolff Limited, Belfast, Northern Ireland, 1955. 16,310 gross tons; 533 feet long; 69 feet wide. Doxford diesels, twin screw. Service speed 17 knots. 512 maximum cruise passengers.]

OCEAN PRINCESS. Built as an experimental cruise ship, the *Italia* was chartered by Costa Cruises in 1973 and bought outright by them four years later. She was sold to Ocean Cruise Lines in 1983 and renamed *Ocean Princess (above)*. She ran aground during an Amazon River cruise on March 1, 1993, and was badly damaged. There was flooding on two passenger decks and in the engine room, and she was thought to be a complete loss. Taken to Greece, the ship was repaired and renamed *Sea Prince*, but then suffered a fire in May 1995. Afterward, she was resold to other Greek buyers, Louis Cruise Lines, and became the *Sapphire*. [Built by Cantieri Navale Felszegi, Trieste, Italy, 1967. 12,218 gross tons; 490 feet long; 68 feet wide. Sulzer diesels, twin screw. Service speed 20 knots. 476 cruise passengers.]

AMERICAN STAR. "Like the *Homeric* and the *Britanis*, the *America* was very solid and was designed and built to go on forever," according to Steven Winograd. "She was one of the most beautiful American liners and, on the inside, was far more elegant than the larger, far faster *United States.* Many travelers preferred the *America.* She had style, those linoleum floors, and was always immaculate. The *United States* was usually a sellout, but the *America* was very popular in her own right." Frank Trumbour added, "The *America* was a warm and comfortable-looking ship.

Her lines were classic, but the somewhat tenuous look of her funnels made her seem vulnerable. Her lovely 1940 interior seemed to be the inspiration for all postwar film noir sets." Completed in July 1940 as the *America*, she was called to war duties soon afterward and sailed as the USS *West Point*. She was restored in 1946 and sailed as the *America (opposite, top)* until 1964 when she was sold to Chandris Lines and became their *Australis* for Europe-Australia service. In 1978, she was renamed *America* and used for cruising, then renamed *Italis* later that same year for further cruising. Laid up in Greece in 1979, she was sold a year later and renamed *Noga* and then *Alferdoss* in 1984. She was renamed yet again in 1994, as *American Star*, for use as a hotel ship in Bangkok. On January 18, 1994, while being towed around Africa and bound for Thailand, the ship was wrecked off the Canary Islands. Abandoned, she later broke in half *(opposite, bottom)*.

"The former *America* is disintegrating. By the winter of 2005, her fore section is just dissolving into the sea. The aft is long gone, having slipped into the choppy Atlantic," added Captain McNamara. [Built by Newport News Shipbuilding & Dry Dock Company, Newport News, Virginia, 1940. 33,350 gross tons as built; 723 feet long; 93 feet wide. Steam turbines, twin screw. Service speed 23 knots. 2,258 maximum passengers in 1965.]

PALLAS ATHENA. "The *Flandre* had a special following at French Line because she had a small, clubby atmosphere," noted Steven Winograd. "She was a rather beautiful ship, but capped by a low, disappointing funnel. But, in ways, she looked like a racer. Her superstructure was pushed back further than usual. Her sister, the *Antilles*, with a taller funnel, looked far better, however. The *Flandre* was, of course, elegant and well maintained, and offered great French food. Her suites were disappointing, however, because they were too small against the standards of the French Line. Actually, she had better first-class cabins."

Used on the North Atlantic between Le Havre and New York, together with the celebrated *Liberté* and *Ile de France*, she is seen here (*above*) arriving in New York for the first time, with the *Queen Mary* behind in July 1952. This ship finished her French Line career in Caribbean service. In 1968 she was sold to become Costa Line's *Carla C.* Sold to Greece's Epirotiki Lines in 1992 and renamed *Pallas Athena*, she caught fire on on March 24, 1994—the eve of her departure for an eastern Mediterranean cruise—while docked at Piraeus, Greece. Still smoldering, she was towed to open waters and written off as a complete loss (*below*). Her remains were later towed to Aliaga in Turkey for scrapping. [Built by Ateliers et Chantiers de France, Dunkirk, France, 1952. 19,975 gross tons; 600 feet long; 80 feet wide. Werkspor diesels, twin screw. Service speed 19 knots. 754 all-first-class passengers.]

ACHILLE LAURO. "She was a splendid ship in design and comfort and revolutionary in engine layout," noted Dr. Nico Guns. Built as the *Willem Ruys* for Royal Rotterdam Lloyd's Rotterdam-Jakarta service, she is seen here at Rotterdam (**above**). The ship was later sold to Italy's Lauro Line in 1964 and rebuilt as the *Achille Lauro* for Europe-Australia sailings (**below**). Later used as a cruise ship, she was the target of a headline-making terrorist attack in the eastern Mediterranean in October 1985. While bound for South Africa on November 30, 1994, she caught fire off Somalia and sank two days later. Two were lost. [Built by De Schelde Shipyard, Flushing, Holland, 1938-47. 23,629 gross tons; 631 feet long; 82 feet wide. Sulzer diesels, twin screw. 1,652 maximum passengers; approximately 900 one-class cruise passengers.]

ROMANTICA. Built as the combination-style *Huascaran* for Hamburg America Line's South American service, she was ceded to Canada after World War II and sailed as the *Beaverbrae* for Canadian Pacific until sold in 1954 to Italy's Cogedar Line. Renamed *Aurelia,* she was used in Europe-Australia service until switched to cruising under Chandris Cruises' banner beginning in 1970, and renamed *Romanza.* In 1996, she was sold to Ambassador Cruises and renamed *Romantica (above).* The ship had close to sixty years service when she burned out during a cruise in the eastern Mediterranean on October 4, 1997 *(below).* The remains were scrapped at Alexandria. [Built by Blohm & Voss Shipbuilders, Hamburg, Germany, 1939. 10,480 gross tons; 487 feet long; 60 feet wide. Diesel-electric, single screw. Service speed 17 knots. 1,124 all-tourist-class passengers by 1955.]

CONSTITUTION. "The *Constitution* [*above*] was very exciting. She had a great name as well. In ways, she was actually more fabulous than the *Independence*," according to Steven Winograd. "She had the name of a great liner that, quite romantically, carried you off to faraway places. She herself created excitement. She also had great departures: the whistles, streamers, and huge crowds. Once, relatives of mine sailed for Europe aboard her, but from Hoboken because there was a strike. It was a departure I shall never forget!" Charles Howland added, "The *Constitution* sank on the way to the breakers after a long and successful career. In that way she had a kind of Viking funeral, and for a ship like her, it is impossible to mourn. She did exactly what her designers had in mind, happily transporting passengers for something like forty years. What a record!"

Built for American Export Lines' New York–Mediterranean run, she was decommissioned in 1968, laid up, and sold to C. Y. Tung in 1974. Renamed *Oceanic Constitution*, she was moved to Hong Kong, but remained inactive until restored in 1982 for Hawaiian cruise service, together with her sister *Independence*. Laid up in 1996, she was sold to Far Eastern scrappers and sank off Hawaii while empty and under tow on November 17, 1997. [Built by Bethlehem Steel Corporation, Quincy, Massachusetts, 1951. 30,293 gross tons; 683 feet long; 89 feet wide. Steam turbines, twin screw. Service speed 23 knots. 1,100 maximum passengers.]

SUN VISTA. When she and her twin sister, the *Guglielmo Marconi*, were built, in the early 1960s, Italian shipyards were in the midst of a golden era. Shipbuilders in Genoa and in Monfalcone were producing some of the most handsome, beautifully decorated, and generally most advanced liners of the day. There were classics like the *Michelangelo*, *Raffaello*, and *Leonardo da Vinci* for the Italian Line; the innovative *Oceanic* for the Home Lines; and the largest liner yet for the Costa Line, the *Eugenio C.* But there was still another pair that garnered lots of attention and well deserved praises: the sisters *Galileo Galilei* and the aforementioned *Guglielmo Marconi*. Both ships later went on to other lives, other notations. In June 1990 I was aboard a New York harbor tug that welcomed the onetime *Galileo Galilei*, renamed *Meridian* by her Chandris owners, arriving from a complete makeover (*above*).

Used on the Europe-Australia service until 1975, the *Galileo Galilei* later did a stint in Italian cruising, but then was sold to Chandris Cruises in 1983, who sailed her as the abbreviated *Galileo*. She was rebuilt in 1989, modernized and renamed

Meridian for the new Chandris subsidiary, Celebrity Cruises.

The "new" *Meridian* divided her time between seven-day cruises (July through September) from New York to Bermuda and the remainder out of Port Everglades on week-long trips to Antigua, St. Thomas, and Nassau. But as Chandris-Celebrity introduced the new 70,600-ton "Century class" beginning in 1995 and then planned for the 91,000-ton "Millennium class" of 2000, the *Meridian* became something of the misplaced child. She was sold in 1998 to Far East buyers, Sun Cruises, who wanted her for Southeast Asian service out of Singapore. Renamed *Sun Vista*, her career was short-lived, however. In May 1999, while sailing off the Malaysian coast, she caught fire, was abandoned, and quickly sank. There was some talk of salvage, since the ship is lying in relatively shallow waters, but this has not come about. [Built by Cantieri Riuniti dell'Adriatico, Monfalcone, Italy, 1963. 27,907 gross tons as built; 702 feet long; 94 feet wide. Steam turbines, twin screw. Service speed 24 knots. 1,750 passengers as built (156 first class, 1,594 tourist class).]

REGENT SEA. The *Regent Sea* (formerly the *Gripsholm*) was unquestionably one of the very finest liners of her time, whether in two-class service on the North Atlantic between New York, Copenhagen, and Gothenburg, or as a one-class, globe-roaming cruise ship. She always looked sleek, like a big white yacht. There were two canted funnels, a sharply raked bow, and a perfectly balanced order to her outer, upper decks. She was every inch the Nordic beauty, the ideal ocean liner. Maintenance was always precise, everything shined that should shine. Within, she was all charm and coziness, like an oversized country club. Her colors and tones were light, warm, and inviting. Her reputation was flawless and certainly envied, and even to this day is highly remembered. "The *Gripsholm* was one of the best-looking liners and was so typical of the very fine Swedish American Line," noted Steven Winograd. "She had perfect foursquare. She had perfect design. She also had a very loyal following, one that continued even after the newer, finer *Kungsholm* arrived in 1966. There were many that preferred the *Gripsholm*. Many New York travelers sailed only on Swedish American Line, and arrived at Pier 97 in limousines."

"She made rather unique history in the annals of the Port of New York," recalled Fred Rodriguez. "A tanker and a container ship had a fiery collision underneath the Verrazano-Narrows Bridge on a June night in 1973. So, the port entrance was closed for a short time afterward. The *Gripsholm* was arriving the next morning and, as an alternate, sailed completely around Staten Island and then passed through the Kill van Kull before entering the Upper Bay and the Hudson River. This was a unique arrival for a liner of almost any size. In 1989, I visited her while she was in dry dock in Brooklyn's Eire Basin and later recall her going over to Port Newark, New Jersey, to load supplies, which had been delivered by containers."

In 1975 the *Gripsholm* went on to become the *Navarino* for Karageorgis Cruises. She did sailings in the Mediterranean, to South America, and even to South Africa. She seemed to be a success, earning a pleasant reputation. But then she was for sale again, in the fall of 1981, and passed to Finnish interests, who wanted her for Miami-Caribbean cruises for their Commodore Cruise Lines' subsidiary. This plan never came to pass, however. On November 26 just hours before the official transfer papers were signed, she capsized in a Greek floating dock. To some, she seemed a complete loss. She was repaired, however, supposedly to become the Italian-owned *Samantha*, but instead resumed sailing in 1984 as the *Regent Sea* for Greek-owned Regency Cruises.

When Regency collapsed in 1995, the *Regent Sea* was laid up and later became the *Splash*, an intended casino ship that never materialized. Her final name, *Sea*, remained. She is seen here (***below***) laid up at Tampa on February 27, 2001. Despite rumors that she might be sold to Swedish interests for use as a hotel ship in Stockholm harbor, she was in fact sold to Indian ship breakers. But while under tow from Tampa to Alang via South Africa, she sank off the West African coast on July 12, 2001. [Built by Ansaldo Shipyard, Genoa, Italy, 1957. 17,391 gross tons; 631 feet long; 82 feet wide. Gotaverken diesels, twin screw. Service speed 19 knots. 842 maximum passengers as built.]

MEDITERRANEAN SKY. The combo liner *City of York* was used on the Ellerman Lines' run between London and South and East Africa. She was sold to the Greek-flag Karageorgis Lines in 1971 and was soon rebuilt as the modern ferry *Mediterranean Sky* for Adriatic and Mediterranean services. Laid up in February 1999, she is seen here (*above*) in May 2001. The ship later burned and then sank at her moorings (*below*). [Built by Vickers-Armstrong Limited, Newcastle-upon-Tyne, England, 1953. 15,212 gross tons as rebuilt; 541 feet long; 71 feet wide. Doxford diesels, twin screw. Service speed 16 knots. 829 one-class passengers as rebuilt.]

REGENT SUN. "The *Shalom* (later the *Regent Sun*) was the most famous ship for American Jews," said Steven Winograd. "She represented the hope of a nation. She was the star of Israel. She was, of course, well intended, but too expensive. Many were upset when she was sold, within three years, in 1967, to the West German–flag German Atlantic Line." Fred Rodriguez remembered her as well, from her frequent visits to New York under several names: *Shalom, Hanseatic, Doric, Royal Odyssey,* and finally *Regent Sun.* The *Shalom* is shown here *(above)* arriving at New York's Pier 32 on her maiden arrival in April 1964. "She was a beautiful ship in many ways and had some very large cabins. I saw her first as the *Shalom* and recall her collision on Thanksgiving eve in 1964. She collided with a Norwegian tanker, the *Stolt Dagali,* outside New York harbor and returned with a smashed bow," he recalled. Her sailings from Pier 32, Canal Street, were always very crowded, almost like a stampede at times. As the *Regent Sun,* I remember that her original Israeli art was still onboard and remained until the very end, and her being dry-docked at the old Brooklyn Navy Yard in October 1995. This was rare for a passenger ship by this time. Her launches, lifeboats, and davits were removed during her long layup at Freeport and remain there to this day."

At one point during her layup, there were rumors that she would be revived: by Premier Cruise Lines as the *Michelangelo*, and by Canyon Ranch Spas as a health spa–style cruise ship. She was sold to Indian ship breakers in 2001, but sank while en route and under tow off South Africa on July 25. This view *(above)* shows her in layup at Freeport on December 12, 2000. [Built by Chantiers de l'Atlantique, St. Nazaire, France, 1964. 25,320 gross tons; 629 feet long; 82 feet wide. Steam turbines, twin screw. Service speed 20 knots. 945 maximum cruise passengers.]

COPA CASINO. Built for the booming transatlantic passenger trade of the 1950s as Holland America Line's *Ryndam*, this vessel was actually intended to be a sixty-passenger combination ship, the *Dinteldyk*. Used as the student ship *Waterman* in 1968, she reverted to the name *Ryndam* until sold, in 1972, to become Epirotiki Lines' *Atlas*. Greatly rebuilt and modernized, she ran mostly eastern Mediterranean cruises. She became the casino ship *Pride of Mississippi* in 1988, sailing on short cruises from Galveston. Her name changed to *Pride of Galveston* in 1991 until she became the *Copa Casino* in 1994, and was moored fulltime at Gulfport, Mississippi. Sold to scrappers in the winter of 2003, she was placed under tow for the long voyage from Mobile (seen here [*below*] in a view dated February 10, 2003) to Alang in India, when she sank off the Dominican Republic that April. [Built by Wilton-Fijenoord Shipyard, Schiedam, Holland, 1951. 15,051 gross tons; 510 feet long (as rebuilt); 69 feet wide. Steam turbines, single screw. Service speed 16 knots. 731 cruise passengers as rebuilt.]

SEA BREEZE. As the first new build for Italy's Costa Line, the *Federico C* was created for the booming Italy–South America service. She is seen here *(above)* departing from Genoa with the *Bianca C* to the left. Sold to Premier Cruise Lines in 1983, she became the *Starship Royale*, and then changed hands again, in 1989, becoming the *Sea Breeze* for Dolphin Cruise Lines. In 1998 she was sailing again for Premier Cruise Lines. After the company's collapse in September 2000 the ship was empty on a voyage from Halifax to Charleston when she flooded and sank off the Virginia coast on December 17. [Built at Ansaldo Shipyard, Genoa, Italy, 1958. 20,416 gross tons as built; 606 feet long; 79 feet wide. Steam turbines, twin screw. Service speed 21 knots. 1,279 passengers as built (243 first class, 300 cabin class, 736 tourist class).]

BRITANIS. At age sixty-eight, the *Britanis* was finally withdrawn from cruise service in 1994, did a stint under charter to the U.S. government as a refugee accommodation ship in Guantanamo Bay in Cuba, but then was laid up in the backwaters of Tampa, Florida (***above***). Her neighbors at various times included the *Regent Sea*, *Regent Sun*, and *Regent Rainbow*. By 1999 reports were that the *Britanis*, by then sold to intermediary buyers and renamed *Belophin I*, would be refitted as an Art Deco–style "boutique hotel" and moored along the San Francisco waterfront. Her stacks might even have been repainted in Matson Line colors and her name changed to *Normandie*, a reminder of the great French liner of the 1930s. But as always, problems, mostly financial ones, for such floating hotel projects killed all plans. In July 2000 she left Tampa under tow, bound for a long, slow voyage around South Africa to the scrap yards at Alang in India. She took on water off Brazil, but managed to continue. Under windy conditions, she began to capsize near Capetown and then sank.

"Like the *Homeric*, the *America* and other U.S.-built liners, the *Britanis* was of another era and constructed as if to go on forever," according to Steven Winograd. "She had an incredible life. In the end, she was a floating museum, a relic. She was, in fact, the last twin-stacker to sail regularly from New York." Fred Rodriguez added, "She was a great old ship with lots of brass, an enclosed bridge wing and wooden decks. The engine room was a steam bath, with 125-degree temperatures, and steam hissing just about everywhere. There were spare parts lying about from bygone Chandris liners such as the *Queen Frederica* and the *Ellinis*, and even pieces from American wartime-built freighters. Old and creaking, she was always kept in top condition. The brass was always polished and shining!" [Built by Bethlehem Steel Corporation, Quincy, Massachusetts, 1932. 18,254 gross tons; 638 feet long; 79 feet wide. Steam turbines, twin screw. Service speed 20 knots. 1,632 maximum passengers in 1971.]

ORIANA. Built for Britain's Orient Line, she was the fastest passenger ship on the UK-Australia run when she was commissioned in December 1960. Used for cruising in later years, she was sold to the Japanese in 1986 for use as a moored museum and hotel ship at Beppu. Unsuccessful, she was sold to Chinese buyers in 1995 and moved to Chinwangtao, later to Shanghai (*below*) on November 21, 2000, and finally to Dalian. She capsized during a typhoon at her berth in March 2004. Although later righted, she was beyond repair and sold to local scrappers. [Built by Vickers-Armstrong Shipbuilders Limited, Barrow-in-Furness, England, 1960. 41,923 gross tons; 804 feet long; 97 feet wide. Steam turbines, twin screw. Service speed 27.5 knots. 2,134 passengers as built (638 first class, 1,496 tourist class).].

BIBLIOGRAPHY

Bonsor, N. R. P. *North Atlantic Seaway*. Prescot, Lancashire: T. Stephenson & Sons Ltd., 1955.

Cooke, Anthony. *Emigrant Ships*. London: Carmania Press Ltd., 1992.

Crowdy, Michael and Kevin O'Donoghue, eds. *Marine News*. Kendal, Cumbria: World Ship Society, 1964–2005.

Devol, George, ed. *Ocean & Cruise News*. Stamford, Connecticut: World Ocean & Cruise Society, 1980–2005.

Dunn, Laurence. *Passenger Liners*. Southampton, England: Adlard Coles Ltd., 1961.

———. *Passenger Liners* (revised edition). Southampton, England: Adlard Coles Ltd., 1965.

Durand, Jean-François. *Cruise Ships Around the World*. Nantes, France: Marine Editions, 1997.

Eisele, Peter and William Rau, eds. *Steamboat Bill*. Providence, Rhode Island: Steamship Historical Society of America Inc., 1964–2005.

Haws, Duncan. *Merchant Fleets: Cunard Line*. Hereford, England: TCL Publications, 1987.

Hornsby, David. *Ocean Ships*. Shepperton, England: Ian Allan Ltd., 2000.

Kludas, Arnold. *Die grossen Passagier-Schiffe der Welt*. Hamburg, Germany: Koehlers Verlagsgesellschaft mbH, 1997.

———. *Great Passenger Ships of the World*, Volumes 1–5. Cambridge, England: Patrick Stephens Ltd, 1972–76.

———. *Great Passenger Ships of the World*, Volume 6. Cambridge, England: Patrick Stephens Ltd, 1986.

———. *Great Passenger Ships of the World Today*. Sparkford, England: Patrick Stephens Ltd., 1992.

Miller, William H. *The Cruiseships*. London: Conway Maritime Press Ltd., 1988.

———. *The Last Atlantic Liners*. London: Conway Maritime Press Ltd., 1985.

———. *The Last Blue Water Liners*. London: Conway Maritime Press Ltd., 1986.

———. *Pictorial Encyclopedia of Ocean Liners, 1860–1994*. Mineola, New York: Dover Publications Inc., 1995.

———. *Transatlantic Liners 1945–1980*. Newton Abbot, Devon: David & Charles Ltd., 1981.

———. *Passenger Liners American Style*. London: Carmania Press Ltd., 1999.

———. *Passenger Liners French Style*. London: Carmania Press Ltd., 2000.

Tzamtzis, A. I. *The Greek Ocean Liners 1907–1977*. Alimos, Greece: Militos Editions, 1998.

Worker, Colin. *The World's Passenger Ships*. London: Ian Allan Ltd., 1967.

INDEX OF SHIPS